STOCKTON

SUNRISE PORT ON THE SAN JOAQUIN

To
Nishka,
Best Wishes
always
Olive Davis
1985

STOCKTON

SUNRISE PORT ON THE SAN JOAQUIN

BY OLIVE DAVIS

PICTORIAL RESEARCH BY SYLVIA SUN MINNICK
"PARTNERS IN PROGRESS" BY MEL BENNETT

PRODUCED IN COOPERATION WITH THE GREATER STOCKTON
CHAMBER OF COMMERCE

WINDSOR PUBLICATIONS, INC.
WOODLAND HILLS, CALIFORNIA

DEDICATED TO
MY GRANDCHILDREN,
KNOWING THE PAST GIVES UNDERSTANDING
OF THE PRESENT, SO YOU CAN PLAN THE BEST
POSSIBLE FUTURE.

Windsor Publications, Inc.
History Books Division
Publisher: John M. Phillips
Production Supervisor: Katherine Cooper
Senior Picture Editor: Teri Davis Greenberg
Senior Corporate History Editor: Karen Story
Corporate History Editor: Phyllis Gray
Marketing Director: Ellen Kettenbeil
Production Manager: James Burke
Design Director: Alexander D'Anca
Art Production Manager: Dee Cooper
Typesetting Manager: E. Beryl Myers
Proofreading Manager: Doris R. Malkin

Staff for *Stockton: Sunrise Port on the San Joaquin*
Editor: Pamela Taylor
Picture Editor: Susan Wells
Editorial Assistants: Patricia Buzard, Judith Hunter, Patricia Pittman
Sales Manager: Bart Barica
Typographers: Barbara Neiman, Cynthia Pinter
Proofreader: Jeff Leckrone
Layout Artist: Ellen Ifrah
Production Artist: Beth Bowman

Library of Congress Cataloging in Publication Data

Davis, Olive.
    Stockton: sunrise port on the San Joaquin.

    Bibliography: p. 156
    Includes index.
    1. Stockton (Calif.) — History. 2. Stockton (Calif.) —
Description.   3. Stockton (Calif.) — Industries.
I. Greater Stockton Chamber of Commerce. II. Title.
F869.S8D38 1984   979.4'55   84-5205
ISBN 0-89781-093-7

CONTENTS

Frontispiece
The expansive and developing nature of the inland port is shown here in this 1870s view of Stockton, originally rendered by Augustus Koch. Courtesy, Amon Carter Museum

INTRODUCTION

Stockton is a modern commercial center influenced by both land and water. The land is the rich soil of the delta and the Great Valley of California, which makes it the center of the most diversified agricultural area in the world. The water is provided by the mighty San Joaquin River and the California Delta, which links Stockton to San Francisco Bay and the sea.

This book is written for the general public to encourage a better understanding of this unique place. Stockton has always been a supply base, even for the California native before the appearance of the white man. It became a transportation hub for riverboats and pack animals during the Gold Rush. Later railroads and modern highways reversed the flow of supplies toward instead of *from* the outside world.

Stockton has been a city populated by those who recognized needs and were inventive enough to serve those needs. Captain Charles M. Weber, the city founder, was a man of vision ahead of his time. There have been conflicts, for Stockton has often been a city without strong leadership, a place where everyone had a voice. It is a cosmopolitan city, accepting large influxes of people who were absorbed yet remain identifiable, adding to the rich social fabric.

It has been a city heavily influenced by world events. Yet in turn it has had a strong influence on the outside world. Farm machinery developed locally helped change world agriculture. The birth of the tank shortened World War I, and during World War II Stockton became "the supply base of the Pacific."

The port that greeted the '49ers now docks ships that carry the products of the Great Valley to distant lands. In recent years the delta waterways have turned into a recreational paradise. Now modern homes use the abundance of water to enhance everyday life. Stockton is a pleasant place in which to live, with a mild climate and rich soil. It is a productive city and a place of opportunity, for it is also a growing city.

History tells of what went before but it can also help one to understand the present. This book will have served its purpose if it does this in a small way.

Olive Davis
Stockton, California

ACKNOWLEDGMENTS

This book would not have been possible without the assistance of many institutions and individuals. At the head of the list in providing references and graphic material is the Stockton Public Library, under Director Ursula Meyers and her staff, especially librarian Isabel Benson, in the reference department. The California Room Collection in the library is outstanding for local research. The Holt-Atherton Pacific Center for Western Studies, under Dr. John Bloom, and the San Joaquin County Museum, under Director Michael Bennett and assistant Debbie Mastel, also contributed with both reference and graphic material.

Reference material was provided by the California State Library California Collection, the State Law Library, and the San Joaquin County Library. The Stockton Community Development Department proved to be an excellent resource. Individual collections of resource and graphic material filled the gap where other material was not available. These included materials from Estella Magnuson, Carol Grunsky, Lillian B. Steel, Delmar McCombs, Jr., and the San Joaquin Delta History Class, Glen Kennedy, and Tillio Boggiano. A special thanks goes to Bonnie Davis who acted as a reader and kept the author on track, and to Dr. James Shebl who read the final manuscript for historical content. Others who gave support and assistance were D. David Smith, Dean DeCarli, Ilka Hartmann, Stuart Gibbons, Gunter Konold, Gerald Sperry, Elizabeth Davis, and Jean Cain.

Those institutions and persons who assisted with illustrations alone were equally important to the finished book. These include: the Amon Carter Museum in Fort Worth, Texas; the Bancroft Library in Berkeley, California; the Haggin Pioneer Museum in Stockton, California; and the Stockton Development Center under Neal Starr.

Private collections provided many of the previously unpublished illustrations in this volume. These include the collections of Mrs. John Kennedy Cahill, Mary Ann Lawrence, Glenn A. Kennedy, Betty Galli, Richard S. Minnick, Sr., Mel Bennett, Mrs. Victor Stamper, Tom Shephard, and Dr. Maynard Lang.

I.

TRAPPERS, TRADERS, AND SETTLERS

A farmer toiling in his field looks up and sees the superstructure of an ocean vessel as it steams far from the sea on the placid San Joaquin River. The river turns southward but the ship heads into the channel toward the sunrise. It travels the route of thousands of '49ers who rushed to the promised land for California gold. The ocean-going ship reaches port at a city 70 nautical miles east of the Golden Gate. Commuters, caught up in the early morning rush, pass unnoticing as the old vessel nudges a dock at the busy port. A seagull dives into the churning wake of a tug, catching tasty morsels for a gourmet meal. Soon the ship's holds are gaping wide to receive golden grain, the bounty of the land.

The sun rising from the snow-covered Sierra Nevada range silhouettes a modern city. It is a commercial center in the heart of the Great Valley, with a population in excess of 220,000. To the north, east, and south lie fertile plains blanketed with intensive farming—orchards, vineyards, and row crops—and contented cattle in green pastures. To the west is the river delta with almost 1,000 miles of waterways and some of the most fertile farming land in the world. Nicknamed Tuleburg but officially named Stockton before the Gold Rush, Stockton became the first American-named city in California. The unique setting alone confirms the city's slogan, "Stockton, Someplace Special."

The land around Stockton has always been influenced by the sea. Long ago when early life forms were still evolving, the foundations of the Sierra Nevada and the Klamath ranges were formed, while the rest of northern California was covered by a shallow sea.

Approximately 60 million years ago an east-to-west fault line occurred north of present-day Stockton. The fracture caused the rising of a parallel ridge, forming a peninsula which projected into the sea as far west as the present Diablo range. Other parts of the emerging lands of central and northern California were reclaimed by the sea, but not the Stockton Arch. It had risen from the depths to stay.

The Sierra Nevada range rose to newer and greater heights as the Great Valley trough dropped lower on both sides of the Stockton Arch. During the California Ice Age, which started about 3 million years ago, virtually all the Sierra Nevada Mountains above 3,000 feet were covered by sheets of ice. These glaciers ground the mountains away, and, as the ice melted, the rivers carried the alluvial sediment down to fill the Great Valley trough, in some places by as much as 200 feet.

As geologic forces raised the north and south ends of the Great Valley, the San Joaquin and Sacramento rivers took the runoff waters to the sea via the Carquinez Strait and San Francisco Bay. Where the rivers met they came under the influence of the Pacific tides that flowed in through the strait. This slowed the flow of both rivers and a huge delta marsh developed in the valley west and northwest of the future Stockton site.

Like all delta land, the San Joaquin-Sacramento Delta was rich in all the materials necessary to support lush vegetation. Both birds and animals, the descendants of ice-age survivors, flourished as the delta teemed with life.

This engraving of Charles M. Weber captures Stockton's founder at the height of his influence, benevolence, and prosperity. His generosity in providing for broad avenues and numerous parks are reminders of the many legacies Weber left to the people of Stockton. Courtesy, Stockton Public Library

A stone mortar, tongs, and gathering baskets were essential to every Indian household for food preparation. These instruments were found locally during excavation for county roads and house construction. Courtesy, San Joaquin County Historical Museum

Archeological data puts man in the delta region by 2,400 B.C. The people of the Early Horizon period—the first known people of central California—were hunters and food gatherers. Experts believe that these people were of the Hoken language stock (one of several basic languages identified with early California man), and were later succeeded, in about 1,000 B.C., by those of the Penutian language group. This change may have come about by conflict, for some skeletal remains from this time period have been found with stone weapons embedded in their bones.

The people of the new Penutian language stock first occupied only the delta and San Francisco Bay areas, but later expanded into the Great Valley until they controlled both the Sacramento and San Joaquin river lands. Eventually, the original Penutian stock divided into many separate tribes and distinct language groups. Three of these groups lived in or near the delta—the Yokuts in the south, the Miwoks in the central and eastern part of the delta, and the Wintons in the north, near present-day Sacramento. By the time Eric the Red sailed the Atlantic more than 1,000 years ago, an Indian culture was being defined in a place that would someday be known as Stockton.

There is some question as to which tribe was the last to occupy the Stockton site before the appearance of the Spaniards. It is likely that at various times either Yokut or Miwok language groups lived near the sloughs at the head of the Stockton Channel. It is known that the native population—estimated at about 150,000 in the Great Valley alone—was large for an aboriginal people. The land was capable of supporting more people than in most untilled areas of the world—approximately two per square mile—not high by today's standards but very high for hunters and food gatherers who did little to manage their food resources.

Was there an Indian village on the site of the city? Yes, there are indications of at least two or three in the immediate vicinity. Carl Grunsky, who was born in Stockton in 1855, noted in his reminiscences the exact location of a round "Indian Hole," a bowl-like depression about three feet deep, southwest of Sutter and Church streets near Mormon Slough. This was no doubt the floor of a "temescal," or sweathouse, in what was probably a fishing village. Grunsky understood the main village to be north of the Stockton Channel west of Banner Island.

An imaginary visit to an Indian village on Mormon Slough would take us first to the center of village life, the sweathouse, located downstream from the main village so that bathing could take place below the area where drinking water was secured. Family dwellings consisted of a cluster of tule huts constructed of tule mats tied to willow frames. Acorn cribs, built on stilts with woven twigs and brush to allow free air circulation, prevented drying acorns—a staple food—from molding. The visitor would probably see village women pounding acorns into meal in stone or oak mortars.

The observer would notice that the Indians did not put their houses under the giant valley oaks, for although this location would seem logical, the Indians knew that on a hot summer day an oak tree could drop a limb without warning, crushing anything beneath it. Instead they used the great trees to hang strips of meat and fish to dry, out of reach of marauding coyotes and bears. Often the women sat under a shelter of tule mats set on willow poles, working on baskets or deerskins, their full tule skirts gracefully fanned out on the ground. In winter the women wore deerskin and cloaks of skins or feathers. The tattoo marks on their chins were beauty marks much desired by young girls, just as young boys desired the status of admittance to the sweathouse.

On a typical day, most of the men who were not out hunting could be found in the sweathouse working on tools, preparing for a hunt, or simply socializing. The sweathouse was covered with earth, except for a hole in the roof to vent the smoke from the firepit inside. The keeper of the sweathouse started the fire early in the morning, for that was his only occupation; since others provided him with food, he did not need to fish or hunt. As the temperature rose inside the house, the men began to sweat profusely, using the curved rib-bones of deer to scrape and clean the skin. Finally, the men ran from the sweathouse to jump into the waterhole to bathe, then returned to stand in the smoke and rub sweet-smelling herbs on their skin to eliminate all human scent. Painting the fronts of their bodies white to resemble the bellies of their game, and taking their deer or elk disguises, the men would go out to hunt. This method was so apt to fool the game that occasionally a hunter could get close enough to touch an animal.

When the hunter returned with his kill, he divided up the meat among the people he felt obligated to feed. Superstition prevented him from eating his kill, so he waited to feast on a neighbor's gift of meat. His spouse would work the hide into leather for clothing, such as the deerskin apron he wore. Feather headdresses were sometimes worn, picket-fence style, around the head or at other times like a topknot, perhaps mimicking the valley quail. It is apparent that these people were highly aware of their environment. Even their dances imitated the animals they held in reverence.

The tribe's only form of food management was done with fire. In fall they set fire to the grasslands and marshes, preventing the brush and tule reeds from taking over the land and providing tender new shoots to entice the game, particularly the area's vast herds of tule elk.

Food was abundant in the delta area: rabbits and quail inhabited the grasslands and were snared with hair loops; Mormon Slough yielded freshwater clams by the basketful; fish were caught in weirs, basket traps, or nets; waterfowl were enticed with decoys. The women gathered seeds and dug roots, never leaving the village without their digging sticks. In season, there were wild grapes and berries to be gathered. It was a way of life suited to the environment that supported it—and the Indians found riches in the land that not only sustained life but allowed a culture to develop.

Were these tribes of the Yokut or Miwok language group? It suffices here to say that experts cannot agree. But recent studies indicate that the Yachicumne, Chilamne, and Pasasime tribes who inhabited the lands adjacent to or south of the Calaveras River, were Yokuts. Those on the

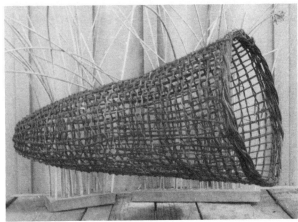

Top: A duck-shaped decoy hidden among the tule lured waterfowl to the Indians' readied nets, providing food for the tribe. Courtesy, San Joaquin County Historical Museum

Above: Indians caught fish in weirs, basket traps, or nets. This wicker fish trap was used in the smaller streams of Northern California. Courtesy, San Joaquin County Historical Museum

Mokelumne River—the Mekelkos, Lalas, and Machacos, were Miwoks. As to the villages located in the Stockton area, the best evidence indicates the natives were probably of the Yachicumne tribe, members of the Yokut linguistic group.

The Yokut tribes were, as a rule, peaceful. They were somewhat short in stature and had a tendency to be plump. Although the last chief of the Yachicumne, Mauresto, was described as a big and powerful man, one anthropologist has described the Yokuts as generally being "round people with no sharp angles."

Early historians agree that the Indians in the delta were envied by other tribes for their great abundance of food. It took strong people to hold the territory, and this abundance apparently made them physically stronger than less fortunate tribes. The Miwoks, who inhabited the Mokelumne River bottomlands, were tall in stature, many of them over six feet in height. Other tribes regarded them as "bad" Indians because

Miwok and Yokut tribes found abundant fish, game, and waterfowl in the tule marshes. Wild fruit and seeds supplemented their diet, as well as the tule plant's roots, pollen, and seed. The tule plant stalks provided fiber for clothing and shelter. Courtesy, San Joaquin County Historical Museum

of their aggressive tendencies. It has been reported that they considered themselves the elite of the California Indians.

Each tribe had a main chief, or headman, as well as a war chief. Thus, the main chief of a warring tribe could negotiate from a neutral position when it came time to make peace. There is no doubt that the Yokuts and Miwoks living in close proximity to each other had occasional work for their war chiefs.

In 1772 the first Spanish explorers looked to the lands of the Yokuts and Miwoks from the Diablo range. Four years later an expedition, led by Jose Joaquin Moraga from the newly founded San

Francisco Presidio, made an attempt to explore the edge of the delta.

In the beginning, the Spanish padres had gone alone into the Great Valley to bring back Indian converts for their missions. In 1811 Padre Narcisco Duran recorded his adventures on a trip into the delta by boat. He visited an Indian village near the present French Camp and traveled back downriver. He wrote:

We had traveled but a short distance when we found waiting for us one hundred and thirteen natives, part Yachicumne and part Mokelumne, half of them painted and armed with an aspect of war. At 6 o'clock we took leave of them giving them wheat, etc. and they promised us that they would come visit us at the mission.

This must have come to pass, for mission records show 118 Yachicumnes and 143 Mokelumnes were converted at Mission San Jose following this date. It is known that many Indians tended to go voluntarily to be converted when bad weather affected their normal food supply. It seemed though, that when they became less hungry, they became more homesick and left the missions. Christianized Indians were sent out to bring back runaway Indian "converts" to the missions, which created continuous turmoil among the Indians of the valley.

In the ten years following Duran's 1811 visit to the valley, the Indians on the east side of the San Joaquin River became more and more resistant to Spanish control. There were many forays into the valley by the Spanish who continued to try to punish runaway Indians. In spite of this, more Indians returned to their native haunts. It eventually became clear that the Spanish controlled the west side of the San Joaquin River while the east side belonged to the natives. This is not surprising, in view of the fact that the Spanish empire had been crumbling for some time and proved to be too weak to prevent the Russians from establishing a fort north of San Francisco. The Mexican government gained independence, and in 1822 California officials recognized a Mexican government independent from Spain.

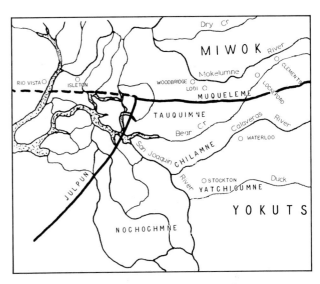

This modified map details the approximate boundaries of the Central Valley Miwok and Yokut Indians. Delineating the locations of the modern towns onto this Indian territorial sketch overwhelmingly suggests that the Yokut Indians were the primary group in and around the Stockton area. Courtesy, Carl Zucker

Where the Spanish had restricted trade, the new Mexican government encouraged trade with foreign ships. Monterey was named the official port of entry into California. Heavy import and export taxes were levied to help pay for the provincial government. Increased shipping brought more foreigners, who often married local California residents. The missions thrived in this era and welcomed visitors, but the understaffed military authorities became uncomfortable and suspicious of foreigners. This was the situation in Mexican California in 1826 when a party of American fur trappers, under the leadership of Jedediah Strong Smith, literally sneaked in the back door of California.

In the spring of 1827 Jedediah Smith and his party of trappers arrived in central California. While Smith and two of his men set out to cross the Sierra Nevada range to return to the annual trappers' rendezvous in the Rockies, most of the party spent the remainder of the year in a base camp on the Stanislaus, southeast of future Stockton. No doubt they trapped along the

American fur trappers and members of the Hudson's Bay Company made an annual trip to the French Camp area to set up summer beaver trapping headquarters. A beaver pelt is shown here stretched on a willow frame. Courtesy, San Joaquin County Historical Museum

Seemingly tranquil, the French Camp Slough area teemed with activity in the 1820s and 1830s. American explorers and French fur trappers used the French Camp area in the summer months for their headquarters due to the abundance of elk, bear, and beaver. Courtesy, San Joaquin County Historical Museum

lower delta and nearby rivers, for they reported taking a considerable number of furs out of the area, including the Calaveras and Mokelumne rivers, in January 1828.

The stories Smith's party told of trapping in California opened the gates to future ventures. The Hudson's Bay Company, already feeling the pressure of American trappers in the Western mountains, sent Alex McLeod south to trap in California. He traveled as far south as the Stockton site, and camped on a small lake—present-day McLeod Lake in the heart of Stockton. The location became a regular rendezvous for trappers who traveled by canoe in the lower delta.

McLeod's expedition was followed by a continual stream of trapping parties in the valley, all reporting numerous brushes with the Indians. The trappers were a tough breed of men, who sometimes made

friends with the local Indians, but who just as often destroyed them, whichever suited their ends. One French trapper, Michel la Frambois, was an exception, for he employed a peculiar brand of frontier diplomacy. An American officer wrote of him, "He had traveled in all parts of the country and says he has a wife of high rank in every tribe, by which means he has insured his safety." (There is, however, no record of his taking a local wife.) French Camp on the southern edge of present-day Stockton was named for la Frambois, who camped there in 1832 and many summers thereafter.

The only written record left by a trapper who came to the Stockton area is the diary of John Work, leader of a Hudson's Bay party of 100 men, women, and children who left Fort Vancouver on August 17,

1832. Within 11 days Work wrote of an illness that plagued his people. It was a recurring fever that struck almost everyone in his party and caused some deaths before the trip was over. The party proceeded into California to camp at Sutter Buttes where they met la Frambois in January of 1833. The illness subsided somewhat during the winter but returned to plague the group as soon as warmer weather and mosquitos returned. No doubt this was the unidentified illness that devastated the interior California Indian population that year. This could have been malaria transmitted by mosquitos, for Work complained of the hordes of these insects that kept everyone from sleeping at night, and in his diary he noted every cooling ocean breeze through Carquinez Strait that brought relief from the heat and insects.

On July 9, 1833 Work set up camp on "a small creek or bay" near McLeod's Lake, perhaps on Stockton Slough. Three days later he sent all the canoes out into the delta for a 12-day trip. On Saturday the 13th he wrote an account of a skirmish with the local Indians. Some natives visited the camp while others tried to steal the trappers' horses. A

battle followed and Work recorded the event in his diary:

Two [Indians] were killed and others wounded, but they concealed themselves among the rushes and could not be found. One of them bent his bow to fire an arrow at me behind my back but one of the women attacked him with an axe and he fled with the others.

They were attacked again in the night and Work reported, "Arrows were falling thick among us." The party broke camp the next morning and continued south. On July 24 the entire party, those on land and those in canoes, convened again at McLeod Lake. Work recorded their take from the vicinity as 45 beavers and 14 otters. He also noted that two canoes which had been in the lake were gone, presumably stolen by the Indians.

Work led his party north the next day. Work himself was so ill by the time he arrived back at head quarters that he did not go out hunting for some time. But it was the Indian population, which had little resistance to the alien disease, that suffered the most that summer. The American trapper, J.J. Warner, later reported that he found the valley depopulated in the summer of 1833, saying he saw no more than six or eight Indians from the head of the Sacramento to the "great bend of the San Joaquin." The trapper reported seeing skulls and bodies under every shade tree. He also found the remnants of a funeral pyre at a village site near the Stockton area. This was the first of a series of epidemics (fevers, smallpox, and other communicable illnesses) that would continue to kill the native population in the Great Valley.

During the next three years the California authorities seemed satisfied to leave the interior valleys to the resources of Michel la Frambois, who spent each winter trapping from French Camp. John Marsh, an American, arrived on the scene in 1836. He was looking for a cattle ranch and had been enticed by Jose Noriega to look at his land grant at the eastern base of Mount Diablo, west of present-day Stockton. Marsh wanted to see the rest of the country first, so he and Noriega joined an exploring party. The group came to a dry stream at dusk, crossed it,

He had selected the location after consulting with the Hudson's Bay authorities in Vancouver. The Mexican California authorities gave their permission for the settlement, thinking that Sutter would make a good barrier in the northern interior between the Mexicans and those who coveted their territory, namely the Americans, British, and Russians. Sutter, they believed, might also act as a control on the Indians.

In the meantime Marsh's letters to Missouri had begun to take effect. On May 9, 1841, the Bartleson-Bidwell party set out overland for California with Marsh's invitation in hand. A smaller group caught up with them on May 23. One of these late arrivals was a 27-year-old man who would become the founding father of the city of Stockton before the decade ended. He was Charles M. Weber, a German immigrant, born February 17, 1814 in Steinwenden, Germany. Christened Carl David Weber (he changed his middle name to "Maria," perhaps to better blend with the California population), he was the first child of Henrietta and Carl Gottfried Weber, the town's minister.

The Weber family moved to Homburg, where the father became the minister and president of the Reformed Local Church Council. Young Weber received instruction at the Royal Bavarian Preparatory School. Seldom near the top of his class, he did continue his education toward the university until a proclamation was issued that all students in public schools must declare loyalty to the king of Bavaria and the Catholic Church. His education apparently continued under private tutoring. In 1836 Weber left for America, accompanied by a cousin, Theodore Englemann. The two separated upon landing in New Orleans. Englemann went to Illinois to visit his uncle while Weber remained and went into the business of "traffic and merchandise," according to an early local history.

Within the next two years Weber came down with yellow fever, recovered and went to Texas, returned to New Orleans, and became ill again. A doctor advised him to seek a cooler climate, so he headed north. He was apparently going to his uncle's but got sidetracked in St. Louis only 25 miles from his destination. He must have read Marsh's letters and

and set up camp on the north bank. Early the next morning they were surprised to find themselves in the midst of an area covered with human skulls and bones. They called the river Calaveras, the Spanish word for skulls. Two previous reports of these skulls had been made but the name Calaveras did not appear on maps until after this encounter.

Marsh was determined to make California part of the United States. He bought Noriega's grant and occupied it in the spring of 1838. Marsh began to write letters to Missouri telling of the virtues of California and inviting settlers to come to his ranch.

In 1839 John Sutter, a Swiss fortune hunter, arrived in California with the intentions of establishing a settlement in the Sacramento Valley.

learned of the Bartleson-Bidwell party. He also met at least one of Sutter's acquaintances, for he secured a letter of introduction to Sutter. He joined the small group that managed to catch up with the main party heading west.

The old trapper, Thomas Fitzpatrick, guided the party as far as Soda Springs in Idaho where the group divided. More than 30 men (including Weber), one woman, and a little girl set out for California across unknown territory, following a map drawn by Marsh, who had never traveled the route. They made it across the desert and into California over the Sierra Nevada mountains through the Emigrant Basin area of present Tuolumne County. They traveled down the ridge between the Stanislaus and the Tuolumne rivers into the Great Valley in late October of 1841.

The emigrants doubted their location until an Indian told them they were just two days' distance from John Marsh's ranch. They were disappointed in the land they found in California, but were told there had been a drought, the worst in years. There had been no rain for 18 months. They hurried to the ranch, where Marsh treated them to a feast. Their host was pleased with his success in getting them to California and he was generous in his welcome. Some of the party went on to San Jose, but Weber and Henry Huber, another German, set out for Sutter's

Facing page: Swiss fortune hunter John A. Sutter arrived in California in 1839, planning to establish a settlement in the Sacramento Valley. From Cirker, Dictionary of American Portraits, Dover, 1967

Above left: Charles Maria Weber's permit to travel to North America was issued in the Rhine District of the Royal Bavarian Government in 1836. The passport included a description of the 22-year-old Weber. He was 5'10", had black hair, black eyebrows, brown eyes, a healthy complexion, and no distinguishing marks. Courtesy, The Bancroft Library, University of California, Berkeley

Above: When the Bartleson-Bidwell Party began their overland trip to California in 1841, Nancy Kelsey, wife of Benjamin Kelsey, was the only woman accompanying the group of 31 men. Although the Kelseys did not remain in the Stockton area, Nancy Kelsey continued her friendship with Helen Murphy Weber well into the 1870s. Courtesy, Pacific Center for Western Historical Studies, University of the Pacific

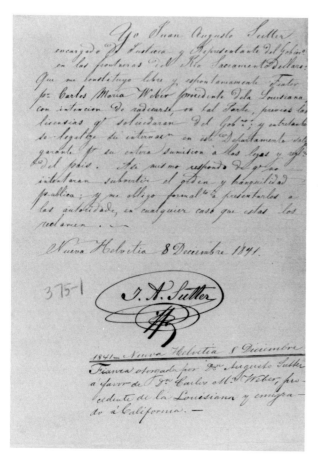

John A. Sutter of Sacramento wrote a character reference for Charles M. Weber in 1841. Weber worked as Sutter's overseer in the winter of 1841 and intended to settle in California. As his sponsor-executor, Sutter assured General Mariano Vallejo that

Weber "would not subvert the public order and tranquility," guaranteeing Weber's complete submission to the laws and regulations of the country. Courtesy, The Bancroft Library, University of California, Berkeley

Fort. On the way Weber first saw the site of his future city, Stockton.

When they arrived at the settlement Sutter immediately hired Weber as an overseer. The rains finally came, and the small settlement bloomed the following spring. Weber grew flowers, vegetables, and tobacco plants from seeds Sutter had never gotten around to planting. Weber first met Jose Jesus, chief of the Siakumnes (the Stanislaus River tribe), at the fort during the winter.

By the following May, Weber was ready to move on, so Sutter gave him a passport to San Jose. If

Weber took the regular trail between the fort and San Jose, he would have once again passed the Stockton-French Camp area. Certainly he saw a different sight than he had during the dry season, for now the grass was green, flowers were blooming, and the oak trees were in leaf. No doubt the game had returned to feed on the succulent clover and new grass that had sprouted after the long drought.

Ilka Hartmann, in her book *The Youth of Charles M. Weber,* describes the feelings of the young man so far from home:

Charles Weber was struck by the beauty of San Joaquin County and loved the oak-studded and tule-covered land. It was like home to him. Weber had no difficulty in realizing that the valleys of the San Joaquin and Sacramento Rivers could become a paradise of fruits and flowers. Similar work to that necessary here had been done in Lanstuhl Swamps during his youth.

Charles Weber soon made friends in San Jose and formed a partnership with William (generally known as "Guillermo") Gulnac, a naturalized Californian who had originally come from New York state. The two men established a store, a blacksmith shop, and a flour mill. They manufactured sea biscuits, which were much in demand for the many ships that docked on the coast. They also began the first manufacturing of shoes on the West Coast, and Weber established an inn, the Weber House.

In the spring of 1843 Gulnac, in the company of Peter Lasson, drove some cattle to the valley. Lasson later said, "Gulnac wanted to stop at French Camp and offered me part of the land. I do not know if he had a grant."

Since the Indians were unruly, Gulnac did not stay either, and both went north together. Indeed, Gulnac did not have a grant, for Sutter issued the first recorded document on June 8, 1843, stating that the land in which Gulnac was interested was unoccupied and available for settlement. On July 14, Gulnac filed an application with the California governor for 11 square leagues on the east side of the San Joaquin River. Six days later Weber bought Gulnac's interest in the San Jose businesses and immediately left for

Sutter's Fort. He sent word out to arrange a meeting between himself and José Jesus, the Siakumne chief. The two met, and Weber laid out his plans. He appealed to Jesus' hatred of the California authorities by telling him the Americans wanted to settle in his area out of reach of the Spaniards in case trouble arose between the United States and Mexico. Weber indicated he believed, as did the chief, that this area was not within the California territory. Perhaps Weber also assumed that his future settlement would be the western frontier of the United States.

The Indian chief suggested Weber settle in the Stockton and Mormon Slough area. This was an astute move on his part, for the settlement would give his tribe additional protection from the Mokelumne tribe. The two men made a pact to support and protect each other, which they both kept.

In order for Weber to own land in California he had to become a Mexican citizen, so as soon as he returned to San Jose he requested naturalization. Soon after, Gulnac resubmitted his grant application. This time it contained the Sutter document issued the previous June. Governor Manuel Micheltorena questioned the large size of the grant application, and wanted to know who else would be included in the settlement. On January 4, 1844, Micheltorena agreed that Weber could be granted citizenship. Nine days following this action, Micheltorena issued a grant to Guillermo Gulnac for "his benefit, his family and eleven other families." It included 11 square leagues on the east side of the San Joaquin River from the river to the "laguna called that of McCloud" [sic]. The grant was titled Campo de los Franceses on the original document.

Weber received his Mexican citizenship from the governor on February 20, 1844, and became eligible to own land. It is obvious that Weber's actions, which coincided with Gulnac's efforts to acquire land, had some relationship.

James Williams, a young settler, went to look at the Gulnacs' grant and made arrangements with Gulnac "to go on the land." He visited the site in late July, and a month later he returned in the company of James Lindsey. They brought 100 head of horses and cows to stock the land and several Indian vaqueros to

Guillermo (William) Gulnac and Charles M. Weber formed a commercial partnership in San Jose that ended a year later in 1843. A dispute over the legal ownership of the El Rancho de Campo de los Franceses, a 48,747-square- acre land grant, caused Weber to produce this partnership dissolution document in court, showing the signatures of Gulnac, Weber, and their witnesses. Courtesy, The Bancroft Library, University of California, Berkeley

care for them.

Two tule huts were built, one for Lindsey on the present site of Stockton City Hall and a second 300 feet to the north for Williams. Within a short time, other settlers, one of them David Kelsey, arrived on the scene. Kelsey and his family had migrated to California from Oregon during the summer and they were looking for a place to settle down. Kelsey moved his wife and children into a crude tule house at French Camp, which was included in the grant.

In the meantime, Californians had launched a

rebellion against the Mexican-appointed Governor Micheltorena and his convict troops, who raided the countryside whenever they received no pay. While Micheltorena marched north against the retreating forces of the rebel leader, General José Castro, Weber and other San Jose merchants, concerned about being raided by the Mexican troops, organized volunteers to defend San Jose. They managed to keep the governor at bay and even got him to sign a treaty agreeing to send most of his objectionable soldiers back to Mexico.

While Castro waited for Micheltorena to do as promised, Sutter decided to enter the conflict. He was no doubt motivated by his desire to obtain certain land grants confirmed by the governor. In December Weber went to Sutter's Fort to dissuade him from getting involved in the affair. Weber was captured by a "Council of War" supporting Micheltorena and headed by Sutter. Weber was ordered to be put in chains, but was apparently left free on his honor at Sutter's settlement. It was here that he met his future wife, Helen Murphy. She was a member of the Steven-Murphy emigrant party, which barely escaped the fate of the later Donner party in crossing the Sierra Nevada mountains.

Sutter marched out of his fort to fight beside Micheltorena on New Year's Day, 1845. He was eventually captured by Castro, who succeeded in driving Micheltorena and his troops out of California. After the conflict was over Castro made Weber a "captain" of his "Auxiliary Forces of Infantry." Weber must have cherished the title, for he used it for the rest of his life, even though he never actually fought for the Mexican rebels.

While the conflict was going on a tragic episode unfolded at the Stockton settlement. In early winter the Kelseys ran out of food and went to San Jose for supplies. Before leaving San Jose, Kelsey visited "a sick Indian." Almost as soon as he, his wife, and young daughter returned to French Camp he too became ill. His wife gathered up some of their belongings, put her small daughter and ailing husband in their wagon, and headed for Sutter's Fort for help. When they reached Lindsey's hut on McLeod Lake he convinced them to stay overnight, assuring Mrs.

Commodore Robert F. Stockton, an American naval officer, forced the last Mexican troops out of California. Impressed with Stockton, who had rescued him from Mexican captivity, Captain Charles M. Weber named his city after the young officer. Courtesy, Stockton Chamber of Commerce

Kelsey that Williams could minister to her husband. The next morning, however, the illness had advanced to reveal its dreaded identity. It was smallpox. As soon as Lindsey, Williams, and the others in camp realized this, they hastened to leave. Thousands of Indians in the valley had died from the disease and even Sutter had threatened to shoot any man who entered his fort with the illness.

Soon Mrs. Kelsey became ill and lost her sight. Eleven-year old America Kelsey was left alone to take care of both her parents. Her father died three weeks from the day he was stricken. Fortunately, a group of herders came upon the scene. They hesitated at first, but finally George Wayman helped the little girl bury her father. He also waited until Mrs. Kelsey and America, who had by now contracted the disease, recovered enough to travel to San Jose. America Kelsey later became the bride of George Wayman, the kind young man who had come to her aid.

Lindsey and Williams returned to camp two weeks after the Kelseys left. While Lindsey stayed alone in camp to tend the stock as Williams went off to Sutter's Fort for supplies, a tribe of Indians from the Amador area in the mountains to the east raided the camp, driving off the livestock and burning the house. A group of men riding back to Sutter's Fort found Lindsey's arrow-pierced body floating in McLeod Lake. Thus the land grant was again unoccupied and showed little prospect for settlement with the double dangers of smallpox and hostile Indians.

Early in April 1845 Weber, now a Mexican citizen, bought Gulnac's interest in the land grant. The document reads in part, "he [Gulnac] sells to the aforementioned Don Carlos Maria Weber for the sum of two hundred dollars, half in silver and the other half in goods, which are to be paid to the said vender at the time of the act of sale."

Later Bennet B. Nell, a friend of Gulnac's, remarked that Gulnac told him he sold to Weber "because the time in which he [Gulnac] was to settle the grant had nearly run out and he could not do anything toward it in time." Nell further said "there were only 40 to 45 days left to settle the land."

Weber planned for early settlement of the valley, for William Buzzell, son-in-law of David Kelsey, would later testify in Weber's claim before the U.S. Land Commission, "I was at Captain Weber's place [San Jose] in the spring of 1845, when he was collecting and purchasing cattle to put on the place." (All Mexican land grants, including Weber's, had to be presented to the U.S. Land Commission after California became part of the United States. Weber's claim was confirmed in 1854.)

Probably because of the threat of smallpox and hostile Indians, Weber did not visit his newly acquired grant. He did, however, by the end of the year, purchase another grant in the San Felipe Valley, perhaps to maintain the cattle he was collecting for the Stockton grant.

Weber was fortunate that the California Department of Assembly confirmed and made official the grant title to El Rancho del Campo de los Franceses on June 15, 1846. It was just nine days later, on June 24, that the Bear Flag was raised over Sonoma, beginning the open American civilian rebellion against Mexican rule in California. Many of the Americans involved in the Bear Flag Rebellion would later settle in or near Stockton.

Weber refused General Castro's orders to organize a California unit against the Bear Flaggers and became the prisoner of war of his former friend. Castro imprisoned Weber at San Jose in 1846, and he was not released until the American Navy officer, Commodore Robert F. Stockton, forced the last Mexican forces out of California. Weber was one of the rebellion's minor characters, thrust upon occasion into a major role. He has been designated everything from a hero to a villain in the affair. One must suspect he was somewhere in between. After his release Weber did accept an order from Commodore Stockton to organize a group of volunteers to defend San Jose again, this time from California ranchero owners. Weber alone was blamed by the Californians for the raids on their ranches, when horses and cattle were taken, supposedly to provide for the needs of American troops.

Weber received orders and counter-orders from the U.S. military authorities. Finally, after he was ordered to give the horses back to the Californians, which he did, he was told to retrieve them again for his volunteer forces. In disgust, he answered, "Excuse me, if you please, I have done everything to the Californians. Let other people do the balance." These words have been taken as a confession by some historians, but one might wonder if it was sarcasm. Was he perhaps saying that since he had been blamed for all the wrongdoings he felt that others should take the blame for what followed? Nowhere is there any indication that Weber made excuses for his actions or answered his critics. He was not a man of words but a man of action. His energy and perseverance led to the founding of a vigorous new city on a major slough of the San Joaquin.

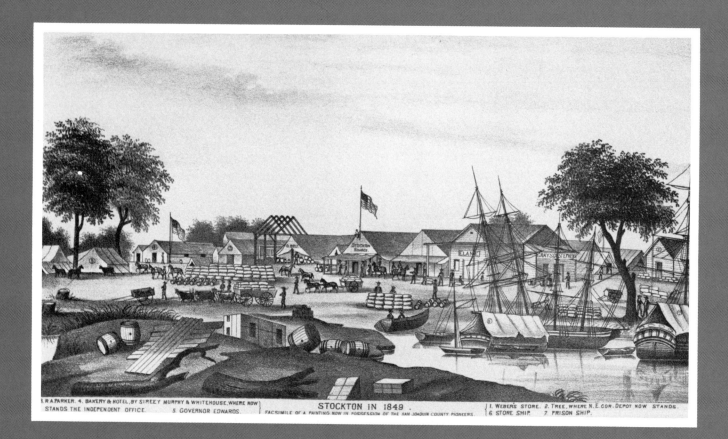

STOCKTON IN 1849.

FACSIMILE OF A PAINTING NOW IN POSSESSION OF THE SAN JOAQUIN COUNTY PIONEERS.

3. R A PARKER. 4. BAKERY & HOTEL, BY STREET MURPHY & WHITEHOUSE, WHERE NOW STANDS THE INDEPENDENT OFFICE.   5. GOVERNOR EDWARDS.

1. WEBER'S STORE. 2. TREE, WHERE N.E. COR. DEPOT NOW STANDS.
6 STORE SHIP.   7. PRISON SHIP.

II.

A TOWN OF "PROMISING IMPORTANCE"

By 1847 the war with Mexico was over and California was secured under the military protection of the United States. At last Charles M. Weber turned toward settling his land grant in the Great Valley. He drove a large herd of stock onto the land in August of 1847 after the river had receded enough to allow cattle to cross. James McGee and three vaqueros stayed to tend the stock and Andy Baker was hired as a hunter. The men built a tule house on the peninsula between Stockton Slough and McLeod Lake in the area now known as Weber's Point. Oak logs were cut and a fence was built across the land between the slough and the lake. A wide ditch was dug, providing a moat around the camp.

Next Weber had a village site surveyed by Walter Herron. A full block of town lots was set out in an area now bounded by Weber Avenue, Center, Main, and Commerce streets. Early historians reported he named the village Tuleburg, but there is testimony to the contrary. Daniel Murphy, in a deposition for Weber's land grant case, said, "I first heard the name [Stockton] in the fall of 1846." There is also an entry in John Sutter's diary of October 14, 1847 referring to two Indian boys who "brought a passport from Weber in Stockton."

In September Weber enticed a large wagon train from the East to stop and look over his land. He offered free land if they would stay. While camped on Weber's Point a member of the party, Ruth Gann, presented her husband, Nicholas, with a fine son, William; it was the first recorded birth in what is now San Joaquin County. Seven or eight families remained in Stockton, but the others went on to San Jose.

Those who stayed on the grant lived in tents and built tule and brushwood huts close together on the new townsite.

Weber went to his store in San Jose and soon returned with a launch-load of supplies for those who agreed to stay. William Buzzell, David Kelsey's son-in-law, brought his family and built a log cabin in the newly surveyed town.

Caleb Herriman was hired by Weber to construct more tule houses on the land. Soon others arrived, including P.B. Thompson, John Sirey, George Fraezher, Harry F. Fanning, and Eli Randell, the latter to clerk in Weber's store. A corral was constructed on the north side of the Calaveras River, extending the settlement's boundaries.

News of the settlement began to spread. On November 6, 1847 the *California Star*, a San Francisco newspaper, reported that near Lindsey's Lake (McLeod Lake) "a town is building of promising importance."

On January 24, 1848, an event occurred that gave further impetus to the development of the town. Sutter's employee, John Marshall, discovered gold in the millrace at Coloma. He immediately went to tell Sutter the news, and although both tried to keep the discovery a secret, by mid-February the word was out at Sutter's settlement.

Weber and his settlers immediately organized the Stockton Mining Company. The stockholders, besides Weber, were Joseph Buzzell, Andrew Baker, Thomas Pyle, George Fraezher, Dr. J. Isabel, and John M. Murphy of San Jose. Most of the Stockton Mining Company men set out for the hills with supplies from

W.H. Creasey painted Stockton in the days of the '49ers, creating a sense of the bustle and activity present within the young inland port town. From History of San Joaquin County, California, Thompson and West, 1879

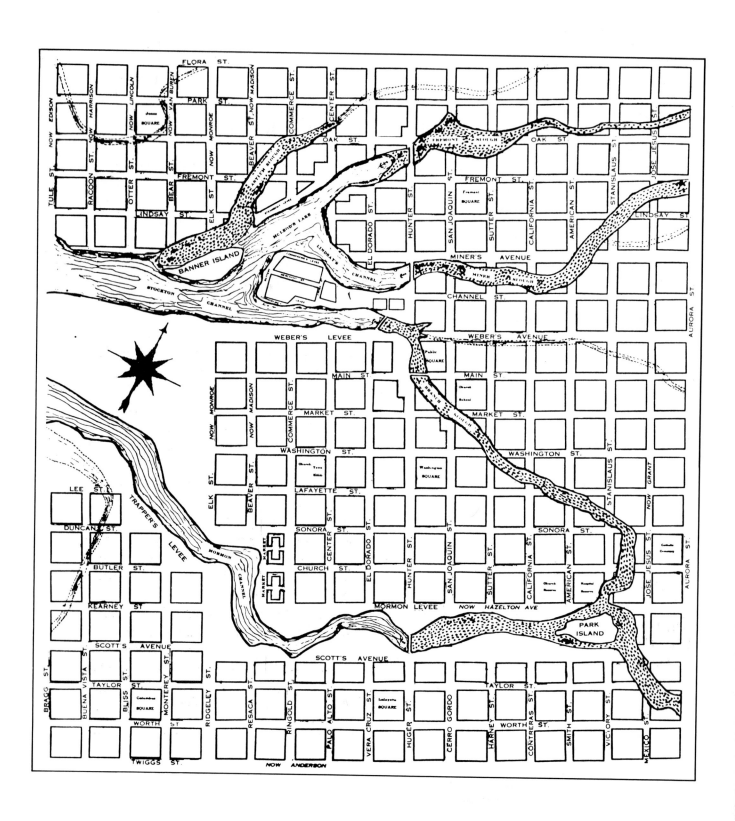

Weber's store and 25 head of cattle, leaving the settlement to the care of herders. Weber went to San Francisco for additional supplies, including trinkets and items that would appeal to the Indians. He took his merchandise by boat to Sutter's embarcadero and by pack train to the hills.

Weber's partners first prospected and found some gold on the Mokelumne but soon moved on to the north. There they met Weber and set up a store on a small creek below what is now Placerville. The settlement was soon referred to as Weberville. The partners sold supplies at a great profit, prospecting only in their spare time.

By June the population of northern California had been smitten with gold fever. Soldiers began to desert their posts, and sailors their ships. California's military governor, Col. Richard B. Mason, decided to visit the mines to get some firsthand information. He stopped at the Stockton Mining Company store in Weberville on July 7 and secured a fine gold specimen from Weber, which he sent to Washington with his official report.

As the rush for gold gained momentum, Weber sent a message to his friend, Chief Jesus, asking for 25 able-bodied men to learn the techniques of finding gold. The Indians arrived and proved adept at the task. They were soon trading gold for goods and trinkets. Weber sent them back to their home grounds to look for the precious metal and instructed them to report their findings to his overseer in Stockton. Soon word got back to Weber that coarse gold had been found on both the Stanislaus and the Tuolumne rivers.

The Stockton Mining Company men and others moved to the newly discovered southern mines. One of the Indians brought in a kidney-shaped nugget weighing 80.5 ounces. The Stockton Mining Company received $3,000 for the specimen from the company of Cross and Hobson of San Francisco, and the remarkable piece was sent on to the Bank of London to show the richness of the gold strike in California. So it was that gold from the Stockton Mining Company, which was sent to the capitals of the United States and England, fired the starting gun for a worldwide race to California.

On September 1, 1848, Weber withdrew from the Stockton Mining Company, receiving a settlement of $6,347. While others rushed to the new goldfields, Weber returned to his fledgling town. He went to San Francisco and purchased a small two-masted sloop, which he named *Maria*, filled it with supplies, and sent it back to Stockton.

Weber bought lumber and had it shipped to Stockton. He planned to build a store on the peninsula, on the north side of Stockton Channel, but the lumber was unloaded on the south side by mistake. Because of the difficulty of transferring the material to the intended location, Weber had the building erected near the intersection of what is now Weber Avenue and Commerce streets.

Weber continued to offer town lots to anyone who would build on them but still had few takers, for most preferred to dig for gold. He had, however, set his course and continued to deal in commerce. He purchased the brig *Emil*, with its load of supplies, in San Francisco and sailed it to Stockton, where he tied it up on the levee and for a time used it as a store.

Walter Colton of Monterey, who had founded the first newspaper in California in 1846, wrote about Weber while visiting Stockton in November 1848:

Charles Weber, a gentleman much esteemed for his liberality and enterprise, is the owner of the land now occupied by the town, and many leagues adjacent. He has given spacious lots to all who would erect buildings. His policy is marked with wisdom; he will find his advantage in the results. His ample store is well filled with provisions, groceries and ready made clothing. The amount of business is immense and the profits would phrensy our Philadelphia merchants.

Other Stockton Mining Company men went into business in the new town. Murphy and Ferguson

This close-up of the one square mile of Stockton surveyed by Major Richard P. Hammond features Stockton Channel, Banner Island, and Mormon, Branch, Asylum, Miner, and Fremont sloughs. In later years many of the north-south streets were changed to reflect continuity. Courtesy, Stockton Public Library

opened a bakery in a tent at the corner of Levee and Hunter streets. Sirey and Whitehouse opened an "eating house" a block to the east on the levee.

Weber's store, the first lumber building in town, was completed in January 1848. (Before, there had been only brush or tule huts or tents, and the log house of Joseph Buzzell.) George Belt and Nelson Taylor soon set up competition in a tent store immediately east of Weber's business. The company of Lane, Douglas, and Rainey also opened a general store, and Jim Davis built a house on the levee and opened a saloon.

Weber must have decided that his original survey was inadequate for a town growing so rapidly, for he hired Major Richard P. Hammond to do another. The town lots were laid out a mile square with the east-west streets parallel to Stockton Slough. Charles Weber was a man of vision. He planned well with wide avenues leading to the boat landing. He also set aside 17 blocks of the city for public lands and parks. The survey was completed in June of 1849—none too soon, as the Gold Rush was gaining momentum.

Stockton became the gateway to the southern mines, located between the Mokelumne and Merced rivers. Every boat from San Francisco came loaded with passengers. Once in Stockton, there were only two ways to get to the goldfields—by foot or by

The Matteson & Williamson plant, shown here in the 1830s, was founded by Donald C. Matteson and stood on the corner of Main and California streets. Matteson, a local blacksmith, manufactured plows, reapers, harvesters, and other farming equipment in 1852.

Williamson joined Matteson's company in 1865. Other early businesses in this same area included the Stockton Iron Works, beginning in 1868, and the Commercial Hotel, which began in 1875. Courtesy, Stockton Chamber of Commerce

horseback. Baggage became as expensive to move as people, costing an average of 30 cents a pound to haul from Stockton to the hills. Needs were recognized, for more new businesses were set up to accommodate the travelers. A livery stable was built by William Fairchild and operated by the Owens brothers. Grayson and Stephens, a San Francisco firm, opened a wholesale liquor store. One of their best customers was Little Jack Keller who ran the Shades Saloon. Two partners, Thompson and White, opened a general store in a tule hut. Isaac Zachariah and his brother set up a clothing store in a six-by-ten-foot tent; starting with an inventory of $50, they made over $20,000 in six months. A 100-foot-square gambling tent contained 20 tables that were busy all the time.

During the heady days of the Gold Rush,

A view of Stockton was something to be remembered. There in the heart of California, where last winter stood a solitary ranch in the midst of tule marshes, I found a canvas town of a thousand inhabitants and a port of twenty-five vessels at anchor. The mingled noises of labor around—the click of hammers and the grating of saws, the shouts of mule drivers, the jingling of spurs, the jar and jostle of wares in the tents, almost cheated me into the belief that it was some commercial mart—familiar with such sounds for years past. Four months only had sufficed to make the place what it was and in that time a wholesale firm established here (one of a dozen) had done business to the amount of $100,000.

thousands came through Stockton seeking gold. One of the first steamers to arrive in the Sunrise Port came in September of 1849. It was a small side-wheel steamer, the *Captain Sutter*. The boat arrived unexpectedly, with flags and streamers flying. The townspeople went wild, gathering on the levee and raising cheer after cheer. The steamboat commenced daily runs on the river and gave the town its first frequent and regular communication with the outside world.

As Stockton became established as a supply base for the southern mines, many of the miners looked for easier ways to find their fortunes. Stockton was full of these men, who either opened supply stores or ran pack mules to the goldfields. Many of those who had been farmers in the East saw the rich soil around Stockton and settled on the land. The first crops grown included grain and hay to feed the hundreds of horses and mules that made up the pack trains. By February 1851 *Stockton Times* editor John White estimated there were 600 persons engaged in farming within a ten-mile radius of Stockton.

During the fall of 1849, at the height of the frenetic Gold Rush activity, Bayard Taylor, a *New York Times* correspondent on the way to the gold-fields, described what he saw as he rode into Stockton:

When Taylor returned to Stockton on his way back from the goldfields, he witnessed local justice. Three drunken men had attempted to molest a woman. A complaint was made to Alcalde George G. Belt, and two of the men were found. They were "seized, the witness examined, a jury summoned and the verdict given without delay." The punishment was 50 lashes for one and 20 for the other, plus 48 hours to get out of town on threat of death. The men were stripped to their waists and tied to a tree. Taylor was appalled at the behavior of the crowd, who "jeered, laughed and accompanied every blow with coarse and unfeeling remarks." Those who professed to be against such punishment told him they knew no other recourse but death. Death was the sentence of two others convicted of murder a short time later. The law was local, swift, and very much in the hands of the people or sometimes the mob.

The Stockton business community became anxious to have a formal government, so Alcalde George Belt, in his official capacity as judge, ordered an election to select officers for the city. The election was held and nine men were elected to serve. But the election was declared illegal by the first county judge, Benjamin Williams, who was elected under the direction of the newly organized California legislature. Judge Williams decided Alcalde George Belt did not have the authority to call a city election. The court further ruled that the aldermen elected to serve were personally responsible for all debts incurred by the city while they were in office. This was a damaging

The side-wheeler Sagamore made frequent trips into the Stockton harbor during its short 11-month service before its engine room exploded. This picture shows Stockton's waterfront where the El Dorado, the Captain Sutter, the Roberson, the Mariposa, and many other vessels competed for the Stockton trade during the town's early years. Courtesy, Stockton Chamber of Commerce

start for the city, making the men a laughingstock for the rougher elements in town. It also discouraged many a prudent man from seeking office in the future.

Christmas Day, 1849 marked an unhappy occasion for the city, as one entire block containing much of the business district lay smoldering in ruin. On Christmas Eve a fire had destroyed the tent and brush shelters within the area bounded by Main, Center, Levee, and Commerce streets. The townspeople had tried desperately to douse the fire with a bucket brigade from the slough, but approximately $200,000 worth of hard-to-replace merchandise had been destroyed.

Shortly after this disaster San Francisco's business district also experienced a devastating fire. The merchants there demanded money owed them from the distressed Stockton businesses, which forced many of them to close their doors. Recovery became a top priority in the town, and by February the business community joined together in petitioning Weber to remove his store-ship from the harbor and to use his influence to get others to do the same. They stated that the blocking of the harbor by idle ships impaired the development of the city. Weber responded, and most of the ships not actively used for transportation were moved to Mormon Slough. Once again supplies began to flow into Stockton in preparation for the opening of the roads to the mines.

On March 16, 1850 the town's first newspaper, the Stockton Times, was published by co-owners and editors Dr. Henry H. Radcliffe and John White. The paper announced the opening of the Stockton House, a hotel built by Jacob Bonsell, John Doak, and a man known to historians only by his surname, Scott. The establishment was located on El Dorado Street on the peninsula side of the channel. The first theatrical performance, put on by a travelling company organized in San Francisco, was soon held in the new hotel. A variety of recitations and acts were offered and were proclaimed a great success.

On March 15, 1850 a group of men met in George Belt's general store to discuss forming another town council. The Times reported immediate protests.

Some of the townspeople professed they could not afford more government, as it would mean "money out of everyone's pockets." But the newspaper supported the move, citing the prevention of crime as the town's number one priority, and noting the need to eliminate the custom of the carrying of deadly weapons by almost every man in town. The *Times* editor, John White, further suggested a prison chain gang be used to clean the streets, work on the levee, and do other badly needed tasks about town. Although the city had no facilities for enforcing the law or retaining prisoners, the county government leased the brig *Susanna* for a jail. Prisoners were shackled below deck, and parts of the ship not needed for the jail were used as storage or for the sale of merchandise.

The business community continued to thrive, and in the spring of 1850 it was reported that $30,000 worth of business a day was being transacted. "Between two and three thousand persons arrived in Stockton last week," the *Times* reported on one spring day. Yet another setback was in the making, for notices were published of the Foreign Miners' Tax passed by the state legislature. Licenses to mine were required for anyone not a citizen of the U.S. or who had not become a citizen under the Treaty Guadalupe Hidalgo, Indians excepted.

Groups of foreign miners soon left the goldfields because of the miners' tax, and mountain businesses stopped ordering merchandise from the Stockton suppliers. Stockton merchants sent a petition to the governor demanding he call the legislature into session to reduce the tax.

By 1850 committees had been organized to incorporate the city of Stockton, and had been meeting on a fairly regular basis. In June 1850 a committee recommended that a fire department be organized and officers elected. James E. Nuttman was named chief engineer, and A.C. Bradford assistant chief. One hundred volunteers enlisted to serve when needed.

The organization of the town council was finalized by San Joaquin County Judge Benjamin Williams on July 23, 1850. Judge Williams called for an election to be held at the Central Exchange (otherwise known as

Dr. George A. Shurtleff arrived in Stockton in 1849, bringing enough lumber from Chile to build the Mount Vernon House, one of the first small hotels in Stockton. Elected to the town's governing body in 1850, Shurtleff later served as mayor, county sheriff, and superintendent of the State Asylum in Stockton. Courtesy, Stockton Chamber of Commerce

the Central Exchange Saloon). The election was held on August 5 and officers were officially chosen in a non-partisan election. Samuel Purdy was elected mayor, along with seven aldermen, including Charles M. Weber, W.H. Robinson, J.W. Reins, James Warner, B.F. Whittier, Hiram Green, and George A. Shurtleff. Others elected to serve as officers of the newly organized town government were: A.C. Bradford, city clerk; G.D. Brush, city treasurer; William H. Willoughby, city marshall; E.J. Edmondson, city assessor; H.A. Crabb, city attorney; F.C. Andrew, city harbor master; and Walter Herron, city recorder.

The city of Stockon, incorporated on July 23, 1850, became a charter city of the state of California more than a month before California became a state.

III.

WEBER'S CITY ON STOCKTON SLOUGH

On October 15, 1850 the news of California's state-hood reached Stockton and the townspeople rejoiced. During the next few years there would be dramatic changes in the complexion of Stockton and all of California.

Business was booming that fall as the mining towns stocked up for the winter. The city council authorized the wharf committee to supervise the building of more docks along the channel. Todd and Company announced it would cooperate with Adams Express Company. The former utilized pack animals (horses and mules) to move mail and supplies to the hills and haul gold back to Stockton; the Adams Express Company transported goods on riverboats from Stockton to San Francisco. In the year since he had first arrived one Stockton businessman, Charles Grunsky, had taken on two partners, and more business, by adding a wholesale outlet in Stockton and operating a string of pack animals that hauled freight to the hills.

Charles M. Weber, who was more concerned with building his town than with freighting to the mines, had a small two-room schoolhouse built on San Joaquin Street near Market Street. It was called the Academy, and there the town's first teacher, C.M. Blake, held class, though only for a short time. Apparently he left to seek a more lucrative occupation. The following spring the Academy was reopened under Dr. W.P. Hazelton. A group of volunteers had raised the funds and advertised "a free or public school where orderly children of proper age may receive instruction free of charge." This took place two full years before the California legislature provided for public school funding and the city council took appropriate action to establish a city-wide school system.

Weber had also begun building a spacious home on Weber's Point. It would in a short time become a showplace among California homes. It must have been a most happy time for Weber, because on November 29, 1850 Helen Murphy became his bride in a Catholic ceremony in San Jose, six years after they had met at Sutter's Fort. It has been assumed that they did not marry sooner because of their differences in religion. Helen came from a strong Irish Catholic family and he from an equally strong German Protestant one. Charles did, however, join and remain loyal to the Catholic Church for the rest of his life. He extended his generosity to all religious denominations, donating land for every church group that asked. He also provided land for the Jewish, Catholic, and rural cemeteries as well as others.

The first recorded religious services were held in Stockton soon after the discovery of gold. On July 1, 1849 the Reverend Samuel C. Damon of the Congregational Church conducted the first Protestant service. He held it aboard a store-ship tied up on the bank of Stockton Slough. It was reported to have been the quietest Sunday ever in the town according to local historian Covert Martin.

A Catholic service was held the same year by two priests on a trip to the mines. During their stopover in Stockton they said Mass in Captain Weber's home.

A Methodist layman held a prayer meeting in a tent in the fall of 1849, and a Southern Methodist Minister, a Reverend Hopkins, dropped in on the

---

This 1867 view of Weber Avenue between Hunter and San Joaquin streets shows a pedestrian footbridge over a minor slough to the far right. The Water Syrups & *Company Building belonged to Charles Belding, who owned the Belding Soda Manufacturing Company. The Belding corner housed the Yosemite Cash Grocery Store* *where the Belding Building now stands. Courtesy, Pacific Center for Western Historical Studies, University of the Pacific*

Above: Competition was stiff among companies and individuals contracted to handle freight carriage from Stockton to the mines. Jasper S. Hall prepares to leave with his 12-horse team and three wagons full of supplies on the west side of Hunter Square, the center of Stockton's early business activities. Courtesy, Stockton Chamber of Commerce

Right: This Rulofson daguerreotype shows Charles M. Weber's home on Weber Point on July 4, 1856. Built in 1851, the house was purportedly one of the first permanent homes in the San Joaquin Valley, and was made of redwood, brick, and adobe. Courtesy, Pacific Center for Western Historical Studies, University of the Pacific

This photograph of Charles M. Weber's family dates from about 1858. Helen Murphy Weber posed with her son, *Charles II, daughter, Julia, and baby, Thomas. Courtesy, Stockton Public Library*

meeting and preached a short sermon.

By March of 1850 the Presbyterians were organizing a church, about the same time Methodist Elder Isaac Owen arrived from San Jose to organize a congregation. The Presbyterians completed their church building and dedicated it on May 5, 1850. The Reverend James Woods had taken a poke of gold dust collected in Stockton to San Francisco to buy the precut lumber for the structure. Charles M. Weber donated land for this church site. He also donated two lots for the first Catholic Church, erected at Washington and Hunter streets. The site was selected because many Catholics—Mexican, Spanish, Chilean, and French—lived in the immediate neighborhood.

All denominations, including the Ebenezer African

Methodist and a Jewish synagogue, soon found their place in town and Weber helped them all by giving freely of his land. The city became more civilized as the congregations grew.

Despite its burgeoning institutions, Stockton was still a frontier town. Records show that in the spring of 1851 thieves were dunked in the sloughs and flogged in the name of street justice before being rescued by the constable. The first legal execution was held under the county court system late in May. George Baker, convicted of murder, was strung up in the hanging tree, an old oak, on west Main Street. Within two weeks a horse thief was also hanged at the same spot as 500 townspeople watched. Though frontier justice prevailed, by this time the jail had been moved from the brig *Susanna* to the basement of the McNish Building.

Culture began to take root in the city with an opening performance on February 11, 1851 in the El Placer Theatre, constructed over the El Placer Saloon at the corner of El Dorado and Levee by gambler Jim Owens. *Damon and Pythias*, *Othello*, and *Hamlet* were all performed during one week. Seats sold for two and four dollars each; all 700 seats were sold out for the first performances.

The El Placer Saloon downstairs became the scene

of an important social event, a fancy-dress and masquerade ball held on February 8, 1851. The *Times* reported the dance was "filled with the youth and beauty of the place." The life of the El Placer was short-lived, however; it burned down on May 5 of the same year. Soon a second dance was held and 37 women were reported in attendance, though apparently they were not the town's social elite. One early historian makes a special note of the fact that "the first respectable dance in Stockton was held on Washington's birthday at the Stockton House." Mrs. Charles M. Weber and several of her women relatives from San Jose attended the event.

Though women added stability and social refinements to the town, they also contributed their labor. Mrs. Isaac Woods opened a girls' school in the basement of the Presbyterian church. Another early businesswoman was a Mrs. Rhodes, who operated a "fancy dry goods store" on Main Street. Zacheria's Tailor Shop hired two women to sew shirts, and there

This picture of an early saloon was used as an advertisement for The '49 Saloon. Partners Gustave Genecco and Paul Trucco first opened the saloon in 1905 on East Weber Avenue near the head of the Stockton Channel, but moved their facility around the corner to El Dorado Street. The business folded in 1919. Courtesy, D.W. Chan

was always a demand for cooks and washerwomen in a town where luxuries were rare and even well-to-do women did their share of work. In some cases young women were brought from Europe or the East as servants, although most soon married and set up their own households. As late as 1859 a Stockton newspaper announced, "Fifteen Yankee girls arrived Tuesday from Boston, a part of a consignment which had been previously promised. It is presumed that they will apply for positions as help, but will accept the position of wives from eligible parties." Of course, there were the prostitutes and those who served drinks in the saloons and dealt cards in the gambling

The first San Joaquin County Court House, located on Weber Avenue near the head of the Stockton Channel, was built on land donated by city founder Charles M. Weber. The construction of the two-story building was completed in 1854 at a total cost of $83,920. This building served as the nerve center for the local county government for 33 years until it was rebuilt in 1887. Courtesy, Stockton Chamber of Commerce

halls. One "beautiful young French woman" was reportedly brought to Stockton for the purpose of running, and perhaps lending some Continental style, to a saloon.

On March 15, 1851 the Stockton business community rejoiced as the Foreign Miners' Tax was repealed. The business community once again received orders for supplies from the hills as foreign miners returned to work. The city, which had suffered for lack of cash, soon redeemed the scrip it had issued in lieu of money and a local newspaper boasted, "Our scrip is the only paper in California that can be quoted at par."

During the spring of 1851 the volunteer firemen organized the Weber Engine Company. The volunteers met and elected officers. The city fathers agreed to purchase a hand-pulled hose cart and pump from Charles M. Weber. This was the first of many fire companies that developed into social, often political, and always competitive firefighting teams.

When, on May 3, 1851, a major fire destroyed much of San Francisco, Stockton Fire Chief James

Nuttman and other firefighters took a steamer to the city to inspect the ruins. Unfortunately, while they were gone a fire started shortly after midnight near the corner of Center and Levee streets. The hook and ladder equipment burned up before anyone could get near it, and the Weber Company pump, manned by inexperienced firemen, was nearly destroyed when it was trapped between two burning buildings. A northwest wind fanned the flames that consumed nearly six solid blocks of the city, and the Stockton firemen returned to find a major portion of their own city's business district in ruins. Undaunted, the Stockton business district immediately began to rebuild with whatever materials were available, mostly wood and canvas.

Despite the town's loss Stockton became the site of county offices, and the history of the port city became permanently interwoven with the history of San Joaquin County. The relationship between city and county officials has often been clouded with conflict. Nowhere has this been more evident than in the events involving block three, designated as "Court House Square" on the original city survey map.

The original county government was organized under the California Constitution in the spring of 1850, with a governing body of three judges known as the Court of Sessions. One of the court's first actions was to inform Weber they were ready to receive any public lands he intended to turn over to them. He responded by issuing them a gift deed of block three, to be designated Court House Square. But the judges returned it to him, requesting a more legal document. In the meantime one of these judges, Hariston Amyx, claimed squatter's rights on a corner of the square. It took considerable legal action to remove the judge and uphold Weber's claim. So it is little wonder that after the City of Stockton was finally organized in the fall of 1850, Weber deeded the square in question to the city alone. He signed the deed in August 1851, had it notarized in December, but did not have it recorded until February 1852, indicating it was not a rash action on his part.

Weber's deed to the city included all the streets, levees, and public squares, and contained a clause that this property be put only to "proper use." According

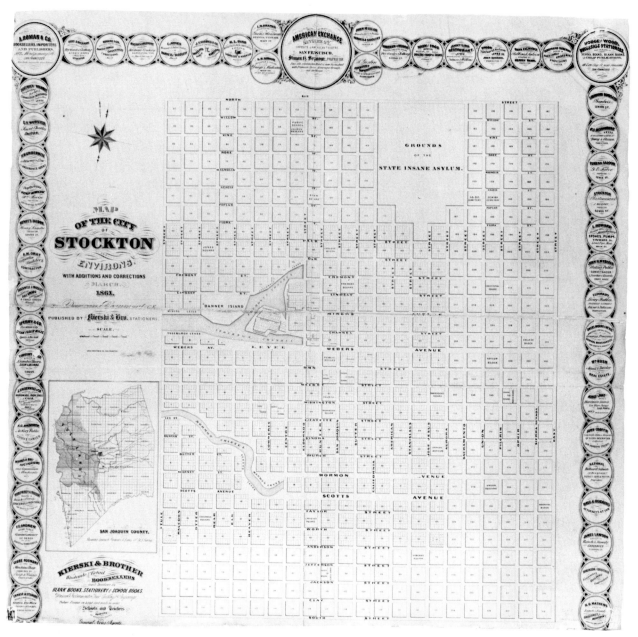

Duncan Beaumont surveyed the area for this map showing the layout of the original blocks of the one square mile of Stockton. The outer blocks' parcels had not yet been delineated. Because of the inland waterway to the west, the town could expand only to the north, east, and south. The grounds of the State Insane Asylum are clearly marked in the northeastern section of town. Courtesy, The Bancroft Library, University of California, Berkeley

to the San Joaquin County Book of Deeds, he reserved for "himself for his own benefits, use, behalf and disposal such portions, parcel and parcels of the different sloughs, channels and bayous or creeks, contained within the limits of the city of Stockton" as marked upon the map accompanying the deed. He also reserved all rights to pass this property on to his heirs. By this single act Weber put his permanent imprint on the City of Stockton.

The state legislature, on April 30, 1851, provided for a general hospital to be located in Stockton. It was opened in a wooden structure on the northwest corner of El Dorado and Market streets, under the direction of Dr. R.K. Reid, and it soon became the practice to send all the region's mentally disturbed patients to the Stockton Hospital. In September 1852 bids were solicited for the construction of the new

state hospital main building, which was to be erected on land donated by Weber in the northeast portion of the city. New facilities were constructed on land donated by Weber and on July 1, 1853 the hospital was dedicated as the State Asylum for the Insane. It has been operating in the same location since.

The rains never came during the winter of 1851-1852, which proved to be detrimental to mining operations. By mid-January there was a depression

Charles Grunsky spent a short sojourn digging for gold in the Mother Lode in 1849 before he settled in Stockton to become one of the town's leading pioneers. Courtesy, C.E. Grunsky, III

and a scarcity of money. One newsman noted money was not hard to borrow. "If one has good security," he wrote, "it may be obtained at 4.5 to 6 percent per month interest." Charles Grunsky wrote that his business profits had dropped from 200 percent to 25 percent during the previous year.

By the fall of 1852 Stockton was prosperous once again, but the rains started early in December and by Christmas the city was a disaster area. The Calaveras River overflowed and the streets became rivers, washing away anything not firmly fastened down. Fences and timbers riding a torrent of water battered a house off its foundation, adding to the debris that tore out two bridges downstream. Charles Grunsky, who had returned to Stockton the previous spring with his bride, Clotilde, later wrote to his family:

I had to rush out into the yard to bring in a horse, water coming up to my waist. The horse, the dog, the cat and chickens were lodged for two days in our lower story. We

lived upstairs. I felt sorry for Clotilde who had not been able to leave the house for two months.

Grunsky, like all others in town, cleaned up after the flood and got back to work as soon as possible. Grunsky's ventures are typical of those of many of Stockton's early residents, for although his business partnership soon dissolved after he returned to Stockton, he took the company farm as his share of the assets. He was doing what many others were doing, looking to the land. He was convinced the price of land was going to continue upward. He believed the land would be a good investment even if farming did not prove profitable. He did, however, continue to freight to the mines to supplement his income.

Grunsky's trips to the hills must have caused his wife considerable worry, for robberies and murders were occurring in epidemic proportions in the outlying areas. Almost every crime was blamed on the infamous Mexican bandit, Joaquin Murrieta. Anti-Mexican feelings were on the rise and one local newspaper noted the only solution was to banish the entire Mexican population from the city. Both newspapers, the San Joaquin *Republican*, which had replaced the *Times*, and the *Stockton Journal*, a Whig party paper, could be radical at times.

The Stockton Mexican population survived these troubled times, but it is little wonder that they clustered their modest homes together in an area east of San Joaquin and south of Washington streets within the sound of St. Mary's church bell. According to one early historian the populace was mostly of the peon class from Mexico. They were excellent horsemen and early in the Gold Rush had been in great demand to run the pack teams to the mines. They also worked on the sheep ranches, and were employed as vaqueros, taking care of thousands of head of cattle in the valley. A few in town manufactured and sold leather equipment for horses, and were part of the prosperous business community.

By the summer of 1852 the city had managed to recover from the devastating flood. There were reported to be 40 blacksmith and wagon shops in town. A reporter wrote, "this class of mechanics are

Safely perched on a balcony on the second floor, residents watched floodwaters rise in 1890. This scene at the corner of Hunter and Miner streets was typical in Stockton when spring runoff flooded the area. Historians and geographers noted that between 1852 and 1950 some part of the county was inundated every three or four years, but the flood during the winter of 1861-1862 proved the most widespread and severe. Courtesy, Pacific Center for Western Historical Studies, University of the Pacific

the most monied men in the county." There were two flour mills in operation. One of these was run by Sperry and Baldwin, who processed 2,000 barrels of flour during the season. A shipbuilding operation was conducted by S.H. Davis and William Emerson at Lindsey Point on McLeod Lake. These shipyards, under Davis' supervision, would launch many ships in the following years.

In April 1852 telegraph lines were completed between Stockton and San Francisco and the operators hoisted their glasses in a toast as the first message was transmitted. By spring of 1852 another new theater was completed, and it was reported there were 60 hotels and boarding houses in town, "all of them busy."

During the spring Weber offered the city the block of property at the head of Stockton Channel for a city hall. The only condition was that the city build a bridge on El Dorado Street connecting Weber's Point, the land on which his home was built, with the south bank of Stockton Slough. The city council representative replied that they had a committee working with the county judges to erect a courthouse on the square and a jail in another location. Apparently the county officials did not realize that the city alone had been deeded the square. The problem was not solved for two more years. On October 5, 1855, the city officials executed and recorded a deed giving the county "one half of the Court House Square and the improvement thereon."

In 1852 the city passed an ordinance establishing the public school system. The privately funded schools were closed, and girls and boys were placed in separate schools. The Reverend W.C. Candus took charge of the boys' school in the Academy. Mrs. Isaac Woods opened the girls' school in separate quarters on Main Street.

Though Stockton was at this point only five years old, the city was well established. It was still dependent on the miners for much of its supply business, but it was also a budding manufacturing center with farmers as well as gold-seekers to supply. As the town grew, the city fathers began to seek solutions to some of the town's problems—muddy streets, unsanitary conditions, and open gambling. Some streets were planked, and all hogs were ordered to be removed from the city's streets. The last gambling house was closed, excluding those in Chinatown, the area bounded by Bridge, El Dorado, Channel, and Hunter streets. This Chinatown had been established early in Stockton's history. In the fall of 1849 a ship resembling a Chinese junk docked in McLeod Lake; it was full of Chinese headed for the mines. Soon Chinese merchants set up shops to cater to the Oriental population. A Chinese fishing village was also established on Mormon Slough.

By mid-century the river steamboats had become an important part of life in Stockton. The city depended on the side-wheelers, and later the stern-wheelers, for the much-needed supplies that were the lifeblood of the community. Stockton newspapers took note as each new and more powerful steamer set time records on trips to and from San Francisco. As

The El Dorado Street bridge connecting Weber Point and the south bank of Stockton Slough was built at a cost of $60,000. Bob Patton, David S. Terry, and John Fisher have been identified as the three sitting on the bridge railing

looking westward down the channel. The two steamers tied up to the south bank are the Amador *and the* Tulare. *Courtesy, Pacific Center for Western Historical Studies, University of the Pacific*

more boats competed, rates dropped and the business community smiled. The competition became so fierce that potential passengers heading for Stockton were sometimes literally pulled on board by overzealous crew members trying to beat the competition. In their races against time, caution was often thrown to the winds as steam boilers were pushed beyond their limits and exploded in bursts of steam and shrapnel. Passengers and crew alike were often maimed and sometimes killed by these explosions.

Stockton's newspapers railed against the dangerous conditions caused by competing steamboat companies, and the companies' owners finally decided to put an end to the problems caused by such stiff competition by organizing the California Steam Navigation Company. The change brought reliable

service, with few accidents. But ironically, the same newsmen who had criticized the companies for the accidents now took up their pens against the monopoly.

In the city's early years Stockton newspapers and Stockton politics were almost one and the same. Elections were held annually and each newspaper backed its own party's candidates. The papers were frankly biased, and heated editorializing was common. But more than once an editor was held accountable for what he wrote. When Stockton's first mayor, Samuel Purdy, ran for lieutenant governor of California, the editor of the *Stockton Journal,* John S. Robb, wrote a series of scathing articles against him. Purdy, a highly educated man of refined social graces, ignored the articles until they questioned his qualities as a gentleman. Duels had been fought over lesser offences, but Purdy decided he would not honor the editor as a gentleman. He declared he would whip Robb and teach him a lesson. He secured a whip, and a gun to back it up, and went looking for Robb. When Purdy found his man, Robb drew the gun he always carried, but Purdy was ready. Using his own gun, he hit the editor over the head, thus putting an end to the matter. The insults no longer appeared in

Stockton's Civil War veterans formed Rawlins Post Number 9 of the Grand Army of the Republic in 1868. At one time the local unit had as many as 500 members. Veterans in their eighties and nineties posed for this group portrait almost 60 years after their participation in the conflict that pitted brother against brother. Courtesy, Pacific Center for Western Historical Studies, University of the Pacific

the paper.

Editors not only attacked politicians but also each other. Two other editors, John Tabor of the *Journal* and John Mansfield of the *San Joaquin Republican,* sniped at each other constantly during one especially hostile political campaign. Tabor settled the feud by shooting and killing the unarmed Mansfield on a Stockton street. Tabor was convicted and sentenced to be hanged in the Stockton jailyard, but received a last-minute pardon from the governor.

As the issues leading to the Civil War widened the gap between North and South, many of Stockton's residents began to worry that the city's strong Southern contingent would cause conflict among the citizenry. Many Southerners had come through Stockton during the Gold Rush, for it was on the path to the goldfields for those who came by way of the Southern land route. Many were former soldiers of the recently won Mexican war in Texas. A number of these Southerners had returned to Stockton from the hills and established themselves in the city. Every newspaper in town—the *Times,* the *Journal,* the *San Joaquin Republican,* the *Daily Argus,* and the *Weekly Democrat*—had in turn carried the cause of the South as a banner. Although the city offices were all non-political, the Democratic party dominated state and national elections locally. The Southern Democrats

talked of forming a Pacific Republic if the Union was dissolved, and on several occasions flags similar to the California Bear Flag appeared in town, suggesting that California withdraw from the Union. Immediately American flags were flown in protest. The Stockton Blues, a quasi-military group of local volunteers, had both Northern and Southern sympathizers among its ranks. Although the group's primary purpose seemed to be to drill and march in parades, the Northerners in the group, fearful that the Southerners would do something rash, disbanded the unit. A new military troop, the Stockton Union Guard, was organized as a replacement, and each member was required to pledge support to the Union.

Both state and local Democrats had begun to separate into Southern and Northern camps as civil war became imminent. Despite growing factionalism, the Democrats remained in control in Stockton. When Abraham Lincoln was defeated in the 1860 presidential election in both Stockton and San Joaquin County, the Democratic editors rejoiced. They were stunned to find, several days later, that Lincoln had carried the state. Local newspapers called all Lincoln supporters "black Republicans." Having no local voice, the region's Republicans enticed the *Calaveras Independent* to move to Stockton. The new *Stockton Independent* declared that it was not attached to any party, but its editorial policy was clearly pro-Union.

As the issues polarized Stockton's citizens into two camps, old friends and business associates took up the side of either North or South. One prime example of this is the partnership of Thomas E. Ketcham and Frank Cheatham. The two had been business partners in a general store in Stockton, but before the war was over they were fighting on different sides. Cheatham

40

David S. Terry migrated to Stockton in the early 1850s and proceeded to bring much fame and notoriety to the town. Noted for his duel with Senator David C. Broderick, the former Texas Ranger also opened a flour mill in Clements, was the senior partner in the law firm of Terry, Campbell, and Bennett, and served as a California Supreme Court Justice. Courtesy, Pacific Center for Western Historical Studies, University of the Pacific

owned the Hotel de Mexico located on Bridge Place where the Philadelphia House would later be built. One early historian says the place was a hotbed of secessionism, and that Cheatham was the underground leader of the Confederacy in Stockton. Cheatham eventually left California and became a brigadier general in the Confederate Army. Ketcham became captain of the Third Volunteer Regiment of the U.S. Army.

David S. Terry, the Stockton attorney whom Samuel Purdy had defeated in the first mayoral election in Stockton on August 5, 1850, had long been active in the Democratic Party. He was Southern born and Texas raised, and during the Civil War he left for Texas, where he organized Terry's Regimental Dismounted Cavalry, Confederate States of America. He was elected a colonel to lead the unit.

There was no doubt as to where Charles M. Weber stood during the Civil War. He flew the Stars and Stripes from a tall flagpole on Banner Island in McLeod Lake. More than once the secessionists replaced his banner with a Confederate flag, so he put a watchdog on the island to keep trespassers at bay. One morning he awoke to see the Confederate flag flying from the mast. He rowed to the island, where

he found his watchdog dead. Weber cut down the Rebel flag, took it back to his cannon, loaded the gun with the flag and a substantial amount of powder, and blew it to pieces. Once again he raised the Stars and Stripes, and, lest the act go unnoticed, fired a 13-gun salute that was heard for miles around.

During the Civil War Stockton became the headquarters for the Third Regiment, California Volunteers of the United States of America, which established a camp in south Stockton at the site of the present McKinley Park. Captain Thomas E. Ketcham, Cheatham's old partner, was elected commanding officer of Company A.

By November of 1861 Camp McDoughal had become a quagmire because of rain on the adobe soil. The troops were moved to Benicia for the winter and returned the following spring in May of 1862. (They had been ordered back to Stockton to prepare for duty on the overland mail route across the northern plains and deserts.) The riverboat *Helen Hensley*, which carried the troops back to town, was greeted with a salute fired from Weber's cannon. The whole population of Stockton turned out to greet the boys. This time the regiment was established at Camp Halleck at the north end of the present San Joaquin County fairgrounds. The troops were made ready and the main body was moved out to Salt Lake City, leaving Companies A, B, and D behind. Company A, led by Ketcham, had just returned in triumph from the Indian war in Humboldt County and the men were the heroes of the day.

Company A was ordered to Fort Churchill in Nevada and Companies B and D to southern California. Stockton was left under the protection of the volunteer guards. Many of those who had taken up the Southern cause early in the Civil War now were gone. David S. Terry, Frank Cheatham, and others were no longer disrupting factors in the community. Many local Democrats remained loyal to the Union throughout the Civil War years, and thus the city emerged from the war on the winning side. It had survived the national conflict, maturing in the process. It was time for Stockton to move on to the business of doing business with the region's burgeoning new enterprise—agriculture.

IV.

THE CITY MATURES

By the latter half of the 19th century agriculture had become the primary economic force in the Great Valley. As more and more families settled on the rich farmland surrounding Stockton, the business of farming became the focus of the community's economic life. The manufacturing of farm machinery would soon become Stockton's number one industry. As early as 1851 a Stockton newspaper editor wrote of the necessity for inventiveness by farmers who would be successful in the Great Valley of California. He predicted failure for those who followed the old farming methods practiced in different terrains and climates—and success for the "men of larger intelligence" who would improve upon established practices.

One of the most significant innovations in California farming occurred in 1854 in the little-known blacksmith shop run by Perry Yaple and Wells Beardsley. They produced the first "improved gang of plows" in California. Yaple was serving his apprenticeship in Ithaca, New York in 1844 when the first patent for a gang plow was issued to T. Wiard in nearby East Avon. When Yaple completed his training he ran a blacksmith shop of his own until 1852 when he migrated to California. Yaple worked for the local stage company in Stockton for a year before opening his own shop with his friend, Beardsley, a wagonmaker who had traveled to California with him.

Years later Yaple would tell how he and Beardsley constructed the first three-bottom plows, with the three plow shares placed on a beam in tandem, offset from each other just enough to plow three rows at a

time. With three horses hitched to one of these implements a man could plow a field in one third the time it took to complete the job with a single plow. These first plows received little public notice and their significance has been obscured in Stockton history. In 1858 Don Carlos Matteson, blacksmith, inventor, and manufacturer, developed and patented another improved plow of three shares, with wheels attached to support the weight of the implement. He renewed this same patent in 1868 when the plows had been developed even further. But Robert Baxter, a French Camp farmer who turned to manufacturing farm implements, must have been a better promoter, for he gained the attention of a Stockton *Daily Independent* reporter who wrote in June 1868:

There seems to be something in the atmosphere of San Joaquin County which excites the inventive talents and develops the latent genius of our citizens. The Matteson & Williamson and the Baxter gang plows have wrought a complete revolution in the mode of preparing the soil for cereals.

George H. Dahl of Stockton patented his "Samson" plow in 1868, claiming it was the strongest of all plows made and could hold as many shares as desired, depending on the type of soil being turned. In 1872 Samuel B. Bowen and Americus M. Abbott, both Stockton farm machinery manufacturers, secured a patent for a two-bottom plow constructed like a cart, complete with a seat which the plowman could ride upon behind the horses. Baxter sold first his plows and then his patent to the Webster

---

Washington School, Stockton's first high school, began in 1870 with A.H. Randall as the principal. The school was located at San Joaquin and Lindsey streets, serving for *more than 30 years as the only public high school until Stockton High was built in 1940. The class of 1890 poses here on the front steps for their graduation picture. Courtesy,* *Pacific Center for Western Historical Studies, University of the Pacific*

Employees of the Houser, Haines, and Knight Company gathered for a picture at the company's Aurora Street plant. The plant was destroyed by fire in 1888. Other farm manufacturing plants in the same vicinity were the Matteson & Williamson, Centennial Harvester Works, Shippee Harvest & Agricultural Works, and Holt Manufacturing. Courtesy, Pacific Center for Western Historical Studies, University of the Pacific

brothers' equipment supply store in Stockton. In 1872 Henry C. Shaw, a salesman for the store, purchased the company. He improved the Baxter plow and began the production of the Stockton Gang Plow, which would become famous around the world. The final improvement came when Matteson invented the first replaceable plow-share. The world of farming owed a great deal to these inventive men.

It is little wonder that the gang plow took on such importance in Stockton. By the mid-1870s most of the town's money came from the miles of golden grain fields that surrounded it. In 1873, 100,000 acres of wheat, 33,000 acres of barley, and 1,040 acres of oats were sown in the county alone. From 1854 to 1900 agriculture in the Great Valley was completely transformed. Where one man had plodded behind a single plow and a single horse to till a few acres, teams of horses pulling gang plows now worked hundreds of acres. The placing of multiple plows on one implement had opened the door to mechanized farming and Stockton businessmen soon were playing an important role in the development of the new industry. The city grew to include whole blocks of machine shops.

The invention of the gang plow initiated the demand for other farm equipment. Don Carlos Matteson and Thurman P. Williamson received patents for improvements on the Marvin Combined Harvester. They developed and perfected the Harvest Queen and Harvest King. Lodowich U. Shippee, farmer, merchant, and banker, put together the

The harvester-combine emancipated the large number of horses needed to draw the harvester. Often the 100-degree and higher temperatures in the San Joaquin Valley took the heaviest toll on the horses. By the 1880s the Stockton Wheel Company's combines made harvesting more efficient on the valley floor. Courtesy, Pacific Center for Western Historical Studies, University of the Pacific

Stockton Combined Harvest Agriculture Works, which built a successful combined harvester. The harvester was sold to Holt Bros. Manufacturing, who marketed it as the Holt Harvester. In 1893 five manufacturers in Stockton produced 450 various types of combined harvesters.

During the 1870s and 1880s wagon trains raised clouds of dust in the Great Valley as they hauled the grain into Stockton. Riverboats and barges transported commodities to San Francisco to be loaded on ships bound for Liverpool and other parts of the world. Within a very short time the Great Valley had become the breadbasket of the world.

The farmers soon found themselves confronted with monopolies in warehousing and shipping. They organized the Farmers' Cooperative Union in Stockton in 1873. The group put up $1,300 as starting capital, rented the Eureka Warehouses, and established an office. The cooperative proved to be an overwhelming success, netting over $600,000 worth of business in its first year of operation. The cooperative soon controlled the storage on the waterfront and became a strong influence in the city. In 1892 it also forced the lowering of shipping rates by supporting the Union Line, a competitive steamship company to the California Navigation and Improvement Company, which had monopolized the river traffic for several years.

The merchants of the city and the farmers of the county had long hoped that the construction of a railroad would help lower the cost of freighting, a vital factor in their economic survival. Dr. Erastus S. Holden, Stockton druggist and mayor of the city from 1859 to 1862, was a firm believer in the benefits of a railroad to the city, and was involved in organizational efforts to launch such a road.

The Railroad Convention held in San Francisco in 1859 had established San Francisco as the western terminus of the transcontinental railroad, but it was also agreed that the first section of the road would extend to Stockton through San Jose. The state legislature was to determine the route east from Stockton. Some planned to extend the road due east from Stockton over the Sierra, thus avoiding Sacramento. But Sacramento businessmen had other plans, and a classic power struggle began.

Perhaps Holden had the eastern route in mind when he organized the Stockton Copperopolis

Railroad. In the spring of 1863 a county-wide election failed to pass a bond issue to construct this road.

In the same election the voters did approve $250,000 in bonds for the Western Pacific Railroad (not the present company by that name) to build from San Francisco to Stockton and on to Sacramento. Although the railroad received $28,780 worth of the local bond money, not a cent was spent in the county. The company eventually went bankrupt and turned its assets over to the contractor, who sold it to the Central Pacific Railroad. The Central Pacific was under the control of the Sacramento businessmen known as the Big Four— Leland Stanford, Charles Crocker, Mark Hopkins, and Collis Huntington—who had no intentions of giving Stockton any of the business they intended for their own city.

After a vain attempt to establish a waterfront connection the railroad was finally constructed on Weber's county property just east of the city limits where the tracks run today, between Aurora and Union streets. On August 11, 1869 the first Western Pacific train arrived in Stockton—an excursion train

Above: The Holt Brothers began the Stockton Wheel Company in 1883 to capitalize on the five assets of the Stockton area—transportation, commerce, agricultural and industrial potential, and climate. The company's employees are seen at the factory on Aurora and Church streets. Ben Holt is at the extreme left in the first row. In 1892 the company was incorporated and renamed the Holt Manufacturing Company. Courtesy, Pacific Center for Western Historical Studies, University of the Pacific

Facing page, top: This view of the intersection of El Dorado and Main streets features the IXL general store on the left and the Holden Drug Store on the right. The electric street car, carbon-arc electric street lamps, and cobblestone road are evidence of the times and the changes to come in downtown Stockton. Courtesy, Stockton Public Library

Facing page, bottom: James E. Kidd opened his shop specializing in house, sign, and ornamental painting in the early 1870s at 228 N. El Dorado Street, and moved shortly thereafter to Main Street. The business remained in James Kidd's hands until 1924 when Joseph Kidd assumed the reins. Courtesy, Pacific Center for Western Historical Studies, University of the Pacific

of 42 cars loaded with visitors from Sacramento. The steam whistle shrilled as cheering men and women waved hats and handkerchiefs and church bells rang in celebration of the occasion. A parade proceeded down Weber Avenue before the Sacramento visitors scattered to prearranged gatherings.

In December 1870 the Stockton Copperopolis Railroad secured a right of way from the Stockton waterfront down Weber Avenue. The tracks were laid to Union Street and were connected to the Central Pacific tracks. By the end of the year the Central Pacific Railroad took over the Stockton Copperopolis Railroad, thus acquiring the waterfront connection it had hoped for. The company also tried to control river traffic but did not succeed.

Stockton businessmen began to realize that their city had become the supply base for all the San Joaquin Valley that lay to the south, and they took considerable interest in the formation of a railroad to serve these customers. There were two movements to establish such a railroad, one by the San Joaquin Valley Railroad, which was controlled by the backers of the Central Pacific, and the other by the Stockton Visalia Railroad, which was supported by the Stockton city council. The Stockton Visalia Railroad had been organized in part to counter the Central Pacific, which was becoming a monstrous monopoly.

The backers of both railroads asked the Stockton City Council to raise money for their projects. When Leland Stanford was questioned about the route of the San Joaquin Valley road and its connection to the Central Pacific-owned Western Pacific, he replied that the road might connect with the tracks leading to the Bay Area south of Stockton. A Stockton committee met with the company to look over the route of the road; Stanford's route was apparently not acceptable, for the city called for a bond issue of $300,000 to support the competitive Stockton Visalia Railroad. This time the bond issue passed and the new railroad was given a right of way down Hazelton Avenue. But the legality of the bond issue was questioned by opponents, perhaps backed by the Stanford group, and there were serious questions as to who paid the lawyers in the case. The court action delayed the project, eventually halting it. The road

was only constructed from the Copperopolis to Oakdale in Stanislaus County and was soon absorbed by the Southern Pacific, another Stanford controlled road.

Nonetheless the struggles between the "Big Four" monopoly (the Central Pacific, Western Pacific, Copperopolis, and Southern Pacific) and the city council continued. Stanford took revenge by building the Western Pacific Depot at Lathrop south of Stockton. Only tickets to San Francisco or Sacramento could be purchased locally; Stockton residents had to travel to San Francisco in order to get Pullman berth tickets for the East Coast even though every transcontinental train passed through town on the Western Pacific tracks. All westbound freight went to San Francisco first and then had to be shipped back to Stockton at additional costs.

This standoff between Stockton and the monopoly continued until 1898 when the Atchison, Topeka and Santa Fe Railroad finally brought the city what it needed most, a depot with a direct connection to the East Coast. The city also offered a grand welcome to the new Western Pacific when it arrived in 1910. Stockton thus became the only city in California to have three transcontinental railroad connections— the Southern Pacific, backed by the "Big Four," the Atchison, Topeka and Santa Fe, and the Western Pacific. Ironically, Stockton was the only city in the San Joaquin Valley that was not established by or at some time controlled by the railroads, in spite of Leland Stanford's efforts.

Although thousands of Chinese were recruited to work on the railroads, they had already been a part of Stockton community life for many years; their customs and language, however, often isolated them from the general population. The Stockton Chinese population was predominantly male, and a number of Chinese established businesses to cater to the bachelors' recreational appetites. Gambling houses, opium dens, and houses of prostitution were established, along with stores dealing in special foods and a Joss House, or shrine, all located in the original Chinatown in the area bounded by El Dorado, Channel, and Hunter streets, and Bridge Place.

Along with prostitutes, gamblers, and opium

dealers, the 1860 census lists the more numerous cooks, laundrymen, merchants, woodcutters, and laborers among the Chinese populace. By now a new Chinatown was emerging on El Dorado Street south of Market Street. In 1862 the old Chinatown burned to the ground. (The fire was not deliberately set, but the town's firemen were noticeably slow in responding to the fire call.) Before long most of the Chinese community moved to the area bounded by El Dorado, Market, Hunter, and Washington streets.

After the wave of Chinese who immigrated to build the railroads had completed the job, they looked for other means of earning a living. The census of 1880 showed that farm laborers outnumbered all other occupations in the Chinese population. Others who worked in town included woolen and paper mill workers, as well as domestic help. The Chinese were willing workers and hired out for less than Europeans and Americans. But in the

A typical wine and spirit shop on Main Street is depicted in the late 19th century. In addition to the sale of liquor, the shop also offered barrels of wine from local vintners. The wine was transferred into smaller kegs for customer convenience. Through the years many of the farms surrounding Stockton converted into vineyards, and a proliferation of vintners in the smaller towns added to Stockton's growth as the area's metropolis. Courtesy, M.A. Lawrence Collection

late 1800s a movement developed in the West to expel the Chinese from the United States. In 1882 David S. Terry, who had returned to Stockton after the Civil War, urged the U.S. Congress to stop Chinese immigration. The movement spread to Stockton, where eventually a petition was circulated to stop all immigration of the Chinese. The community's sentiments were mixed, for a Stockton newspaper printed a very favorable story about the consecration of a new Joss House, the Heungshen Temple, and the industrious character of the Chinese.

It was not long, however, before the politicians needing strong platforms took up the cry against the Chinese, and the press soon followed. The Federated Machinists and the Laborers' Union boycotted against businesses who hired Chinese. By March of 1886 the *Stockton Independent* became disenchanted with the movement when the Laborers' Union leader called for a boycott of the newspaper because of its lack of endorsement of all the union's activities.

It was, however, the farmers who came to the rescue of the Chinese. The Stockton Grange No. 7, Patrons of Husbandry denounced the boycotts as "un-American, unjust, tyrannical and opposed to our laws of free institution." The group also condemned the California press for "encouraging the evil passion of the worst elements of Society." Since most of the valley's Chinese were working on farms, it is apparent that the agricultural community did not want to be boycotted for hiring them.

Sylvia Sun Minnick, in her 1983 thesis on the San Joaquin County Chinese, summed up the conditions in the Stockton Chinese community during this trying period:

It is without doubt the 1885-86 anti-Chinese campaign was the major reason that the Chinese laundry business as well as the other Chinese occupations declined in Stockton and within the county. The campaign itself was not a total success; but the fact that Stockton did not experience any major violent incident is a credit to her community leaders. Foremost in the minds of all those who worked against the Chinese was that any action taken had to be within the legal system; that philosophy, in spite of racist feelings, demonstrates the people's respect for the law.

Ironically, respect for the law sometimes eluded the town's first citizens. In his later years Charles M. Weber, the city's benefactor, experienced frustrations that sometimes led to irrational actions on his part. He had worked continually to protect not only his land but the whole city from floods. He constructed canals along both East and North streets to divert

Facing page, top: Work began for the spectacular wood and glass Agricultural Pavilion in 1887 and was completed the following year at a cost of $50,000. The building occupied one square block bounded by Washington, Lafayette, Hunter, and San Joaquin streets, otherwise known as Washington Square. Courtesy, Mel Bennett

Facing page, bottom: In the early morning light of September 29, 1902, Stocktonians saw only rubble and twisted metal on Washington Square, the result of a devastating fire which destroyed the beautiful 39,000-square-foot Agricultural Pavilion, and took the life of fireman Tom Walsh. Courtesy, Pacific Center for Western Historical Studies, University of the Pacific

floodwaters. He raised the levees along both Stockton and Mormon sloughs and built a bulkhead on the latter at Stanislaus Street. Yet he did not succeed in convincing the city leaders to complete the project. This frustration, along with the constant harrassment he endured from people who tore down the fences around his property in order to let their livestock graze on his land, led him to take potshots at trespassers, including mischievous boys. On one such occasion a youngster broke an arm in his efforts to escape. This led the *Stockton Independent* to editorialize about Weber in April of 1877:

Captain C.M. Weber, the pioneer founder of our city, is a man of ungovernable temper and of so many peculiar and eccentric freaks of character that his best friends are at all times at a loss to know in what new form his eccentricities will manifest themselves. While he is one of the most generous men in the world, he is peculiarly sensitive about being imposed upon and a trespassing cow on his property will put him in more of a rage than would a more serious matter.

Weber invited the editor to meet with him and told him of his frustrations in getting the city to act. He had done more than his part, he believed, and he expected the city government to do its share in protecting the downtown. The editor printed Weber's comments and agreed that anyone might be as frustrated under similar circumstances, but did not

Left: Although floods occurred frequently in Stockton, snowfall was a rarity. This picturesque scene of the first courthouse taken after the January 28, 1880, snowstorm serves as a reminder of this phenomenal event of the past that few can recall and documents seldom record. Courtesy, Pacific Center for Western Historical Studies, University of the Pacific

Above: The second San Joaquin County Court House, constructed of brick and faced with marble, was completed in 1891 at a total cost of $278,850. The contractor received additional money for the project by erecting a high fence around the entire lot, charging 10 cents to every sidewalk superintendent who wanted to watch the construction. Courtesy, San Joaquin County Historical Museum

retract his remarks about Weber's temperament. It was true that Weber no longer socialized and led a reclusive life during his later years. His one pleasure seemed to be gardening. His health deteriorated and although he was in great pain during his last few months he refused to take morphine. He died of pneumonia on May 3, 1881, and was buried on the following Saturday.

The Stockton City Council adopted a resolution suspending all business in the city at one o'clock on the day of the funeral. St. Mary's Church was overflowing for the funeral Mass. The procession—led by over 500 men representing the fire department, various societies, and military groups—marched from the church. The horse-drawn hearse was followed by over 100 carriages. Everyone in Stockton was represented; the last four carriages were filled with Weber's friends from Chinatown. Weber himself might have been surprised at the size of the crowd that came to pay tribute. The populace finally gave him the recognition he must have believed he deserved.

By the mid-1880s the town was growing up, and its institutions, as well as its citizenry, matured. The older men in the volunteer fire companies—which had traditionally been social and political organizations—spoke of the need for a paid fire department. The younger men joining the fire companies volunteered as much for fun as for firefighting. With more incendiary fires occurring, the need for a dependable team increased. According to one local historian, it was the firemen themselves who set many of these fires, presumably to beat competitive companies to the scene. "At some of these fires liquor was freely passed around and some of the firemen became staggering drunk." In 1887 the volunteer companies joined in requesting that the city council establish a paid fire department, which they finally did in August 1888.

Stockton took on a new look during the summer of 1888 when the block-long Agricultural Pavilion was constructed on Washington Square. It was the largest building in town, and certainly one of the most beautiful, and was used for many community activities. At night the lights in its dome could be

Built in 1893, the San Joaquin County Jail on San Joaquin and Channel streets was dubbed "Cunningham's Castle" in honor of Thomas Cunningham, who served as sheriff for almost 30 years. Because the jail was originally constructed to house only 75 prisoners, overcrowding and lack of sanitation facilities forced its closure by 1959 and new facilities were built in French Camp. Courtesy, San Joaquin County Historical Museum

seen for miles. The handsome building stood for 14 years until it burned in a raging fire that consumed the structure within an hour.

For some time city leaders had discussed the need for a new courthouse, but in 1885 the question of title to the land arose once again. The city lacked funds to spend on such an ambitious project, so the county filed an action to obtain a clear title. The court ruled that the land remained the property of the Weber heirs but that the public held the easement as long as the property was used for public purposes.

The ruling declared that the city still held a half-interest in improvements on the property, so a compromise was worked out in which the city turned over its share of the interest to the county in

exchange for 15 years' rent in designated rooms of the new building. Thus the second courthouse, the grandest in California, constructed of brick and faced with California granite, was completed in December 1890 on Block 3, or Court House Square.

In 1893 a new jail was also constructed. The red brick structure, of an unusual medieval design, was known to four generations as Cunningham's Castle. Thomas Cunningham, who influenced the building's design, served as county sheriff for almost 30 years, from 1871 to 1899. He had been a Stockton city councilman and was highly respected both locally and in California law circles.

By the 1890s Stockton had become an industrial city. A California magazine article published in 1893 discussed local manufacturers and their workers:

They employ an army of 1,300 operatives to whom they pay $1,000,000 annually and a large proportion of the earnings are invested in home building. The result is that Stockton breadwinners are largely also homeowners, and the proportion of pretty cottages and even more pretentious residences owned by wage-workers in this city is hardly excelled in any city in the United States.

Above: The 1890 July Fourth parade makes its way westward along Weber Avenue. This picture was taken from the courthouse and shows a good view of the Capitol Hotel (the Mansion House), the Tretheway Building (the Argonaut Hotel), and the Hammond and Yardley Grocery Store. The Tin House and Weber Baths are to the extreme left, and behind them is the Masonic Temple with flags flying on the roof. Courtesy, Pacific Center for Western Historical Studies, University of the Pacific

Facing page, top: Franklin Grammar School was built in 1859 at Center and Washington streets and torn down 100 years later. Better known as Center Street School, it served as the educational institution for the town's ethnic minority communities. Chinese and Japanese children attended Franklin School exclusively during times of racial tension in the early decades of the 20th century. Courtesy, Pacific Center for Western Historical Studies, University of the Pacific

Facing page, bottom: The Fremont Grammar School at Aurora and Fremont streets held a Columbus Day celebration in 1892 for parents and local residents. The school opened in 1890 and was temporarily closed the following year because of a diphtheria scare. The belltower became the subject of much ridicule until it was removed in 1911. Courtesy, Pacific Center for Western Historical Studies, University of the Pacific

Many of the finer homes in Stockton were actually the second homes of farmers who did not want their families isolated on farms during the winter when the roads were too muddy to travel. Town homes also made it possible for farm children to attend the more convenient city schools.

Stockton's increasing maturity was reflected in the pressure that population growth caused in the city school system. In 1870 teacher Ambrose H. Randall saw the need for an extended educational system and started a high school in the front rooms of Stockton School District's Washington School. Classes were held there until 1904 when Stockton High School

This home belonged to the assistant physician of the State Insane Asylum and was located on the institution's grounds. A two-story brick structure, the house had many *windows which provided ample ventilation to cool the residents during Stockton's heat waves. Courtesy, Stockton Development Center*

was built at the corner of California and Vine streets. Among the high school's first graduates were Lottie and Ewald Carl Grunsky, the eldest children of early settler Charles Grunsky. The graduates were awarded teaching certificates with their diplomas. Lottie began teaching immediately and spent most of her life working in the Stockton school system. The Lottie Grunsky School, built in 1919 in east Stockton, was named for her. Young Carl taught locally for one year

and then went to Germany to complete his education. He received a degree in engineering and returned to California where he pursued a distinguished career in state, city, and federal water projects, including the Panama Canal and the Port of Stockton.

During the 1850s the few black children in town had been welcomed into the school system but by 1860 political pressure had forced these children into a private school. The "Colored School" was incorporated into the Stockton school district in 1863 but was still operated as a segregated facility. In 1876 a black student was refused entry into the high school and was sent to San Francisco to complete his studies. But within two years the first blacks were admitted into the high school and in 1879 the Stockton School

District "Colored School" was closed and all went to regular schools. The first Japanese student, George Katsumi Kusano, graduated from Stockton High School in 1895. It was not until 1899 that the first Chinese student, Guy Tye, was allowed into a class, but he was soon followed by other Chinese entering the Stockton school system. Unfortunately the Chinese students would not be the last to face prejudice in the schools; they were, however, apparently the last ones openly refused admittance. As intolerant as this seems, Stockton was more than 20 years ahead of San Francisco in allowing Chinese students into the public school system.

In the years preceding the turn of the century Stockton's boundaries grew to the south and east. Gaslights of an earlier era were replaced by electric lights. Horse-drawn streetcars were replaced by electric trolleys. Some city streets that had been paved with planks and gravel were now paved with basalt blocks and granite curbs. Others were graveled.

As the city moved into the 20th century, Stockton became known for its hospitals for the mentally ill. In addition to the State Insane Asylum, another institution, the Pacific Asylum, was established by Dr. Asa Clark, who eventually became superintendent of the state asylum. Clark was one of many early residents whose contributions helped shape the young city.

The story of one such resident, Charles Grunsky, typifies the stories of Stockton's pioneer settlers. Grunsky had been a participant in the city's growth almost from its beginnings. He had made a fortune while engaged in business with the miners, but returned to his home in Germany to claim a bride, then settled down to raise his family in Stockton. In 1856 he became the president and main moving force in the Turnverein, a German athletic and social group. His early fortune dwindled away, mostly because of an unfortunate selection of partners in a variety of businesses, including farming, of which he knew little. He had also been politically active and held numerous public offices. He was at one time or another harbor master, city auditor, and county recorder. Though he was a cut above the ordinary citizen, his problems were the same as those

During city celebrations in the 1900s the Main Street entrance and the dome of the courthouse were outlined by hundreds of individual incandescent electric lights that relayed a festive message to all the town's citizens. Stock-tonians referred to the spectacular illumination as a "blaze of light, turning night into day." Courtesy, Pacific Center for Western Historical Studies, University of the Pacific

experienced by many men of the times. He lost his first two wives to tuberculosis and two children died in infancy. His third wife had been widowed, and he helped raise her two children. He was a family man who taught his children self-respect and responsibility. In his later years he saw three of his sons marry, and lived to see five of his grandchildren born. Grunsky died in August of 1891, 52 years after arriving in Stockton.

By the time the 20th century approached, Stockton had changed. Besides founding fathers like Grunsky and Weber, settlers such as David S. Terry, Thomas Cunningham, and many of the other early pioneers were dead. The city entered a new era with new pioneers in charge.

V.

CHANGING TIMES

The city of Stockton was undergoing many changes at the beginning of the 20th century. Growth and changes in farming brought changes to the city as well, and the busy port that had served the mines now serviced the farms.

Local farming had begun with the production of grain and hay to feed livestock; later the grain was exported to cities around the world. Vegetables and fruit were grown locally to feed the local population, but, with the coming of the railroads, valley farmers found they could ship produce out to a greater area. Thus new types of farming developed. As emigrants came into the area, settling on small parcels of land, intensive farming became the valley's new direction. Orchards, vineyards, and truck gardens required various types of machinery, so the town's machine shops built new equipment for tilling, harvesting, and processing farm products. Canneries were established near the source of supply and provided employment for local women outside their homes.

Around 1900 a new influx of Italians came to Stockton—although there had always been Italians in the city, for some had emigrated during the Gold Rush. Gaetano Alegretti's grocery and saloon became a gathering place for the new emigrants. Alegretti, who had opened his Stockton store in 1869, was fluent in English, French, and Spanish, and was often asked to write letters home for those who could not write. He became the new arrivals' advisor and friend. He encouraged the Italian farmers to organize a "mutual benefit society," suggesting they restrict their membership to men who were both farmers and Italians. In 1902 he helped them set up the organization even though he was not eligible for membership under the rules. They named the group *Societa Italiana Dei Gardinieri*, (the Italian Gardeners' Society). They soon elected officers and the group began to grow, forming a strong organization that would one day be their salvation. The Italian Gardeners took up farming in several rural locations near Stockton, but those in closest proximity lived in the area between the north edge of Stockton and the Calaveras River.

As the small parcels of land were farmed north of Stockton, the delta west of the city was also developed. The delta soil is a light, fluffy peat of decomposed vegetation, so completely organic it will burn. This land required new machines and Stockton's inventors met the challenge. Robert Baxter had experimented and built a successful ditching plow for the light peat soil as early as 1860. The Samson Iron Works built marine and stationary engines to pump out the surplus water in the delta fields, and the Stockton Iron Works manufactured clamshell diggers to replace Chinese laborers in the construction of levees.

As the need for local river transportation increased, William Colberg established a fleet of small boats to service the isolated farms. He carried passengers and light freight for pay, but delivered the mail free for many years until the company received a government contract in 1928. Before 1900 he started a boat works to keep his fleet in shape and expanded it into an extensive shipbuilding operation, Colberg Boat Works, which became Colberg Inc. in 1960. The firm is still operating today.

A dramatic skyline view of Stockton in the 1930s shows the growing businesses in the downtown section. The courthouse dome on the left towers over the magnificent Hotel Stockton at the head of the Stockton Channel. The body of water to the right is McLeod Lake. Courtesy, Pacific Center for Western Historical Studies, University of the Pacific

By the turn of the century steam tractors began to replace horses, but in order to keep the heavy machines from sinking into the light delta soil their wheels were made wider and wider. Benjamin Holt kept increasing the size of the wheels on his steam tractors until they were 16 feet wide. In 1904 Holt put his men to work re-designing track-laying wheels that would more evenly distribute the weight of the tractors. The first improved "tracks" were installed on a standard steam traction engine during the winter of 1905. Holt tested the model in the delta soil and several were sold commercially, having to prove themselves on the job. Because steam engines were so heavy Holt experimented with gasoline engines and in 1906 produced his first model, Number 1001. A Stockton photographer, Charles Clements, named the contraption when he remarked, "it crawls like a caterpillar." Holt liked the description and used the name. Thus the Caterpillar tractor, the machine that would help change the face of the world, was born in Stockton.

One of the most successful early delta farmers was a Japanese, George Shima, of Stockton. He was a shrewd but fair businessman and was highly respected in Stockton, despite ill feelings toward many of his countrymen due to a statewide anti-Japanese movement created by organized labor. In 1892 San Francisco labor leader Dennis Kearny had planted the seeds of opposition as he declared the Japanese would "demoralize and disorganize the labor market." A local newspaper claimed the Japanese attitude had become arrogant after Japan won the Russo-Japanese War in 1905. But the mistrust of the Japanese more often stemmed from the fact that they were, as a group, frugal and industrious, saving their money and venturing into farming for themselves. They recognized the value of the delta soil for farming, but they were also willing to live in the delta, which was isolated by the lack of roads. Many of their farms could be reached only by water. A pro-Japanese association was organized in Stockton in 1907 but that was soon countered by the formation, in 1908, of a local chapter of the statewide Exclusion League, organized to keep Japanese out of the country. The

Facing page: Unloading a barge of bricks is representative of waterfront activities, the Stockton Channel playing a key role in transportation and town development. Paying only 50 cents for a one-way fare, passengers waited at the waterfront to board steamers bound for San Francisco. A marvelous view of the Masonic Temple, which was built in 1883 and razed in 1931, is also featured in this photograph. Courtesy, Stockton Public Library

Above: Founded in 1902, the Italian Gardeners Society has been the leading organization to perpetuate Stockton's Italian culture. The group's popular annual picnic was held at Bide-A-Wee Park at Wilson Way and Main Street in 1911. Courtesy, Tillio Boggiano

Right: A river schooner, sometimes referred to as a mud scow, gracefully makes its way on the San Joaquin River in 1907. Also known as the workhorses of the river, the schooners were commonly used for hauling bricks, sand, wheat, and barley. Courtesy, Glenn A. Kennedy

state Alien Land Law of 1913, which excluded ownership of land by those not eligible for citizenship, was directly aimed at these farmers. Additional restrictive laws were passed in 1920 and 1923, but many Japanese continued to lease land and farm around Stockton or establish businesses in town until World War II.

Many Stockton residents were startled awake early on April 18, 1906 by the sound of chimney bricks crashing down on their rooftops. But minor damage in the city was soon forgotten as news of the devastation in San Francisco spread throughout the community. Citizens immediately mobilized to provide help in the form of both money and supplies. By the following day a steamer left Stockton with 1,500 blankets from the Stockton Woolen Mills, 600 sacks of potatoes, 2,000 loaves of bread, and several hundred sacks of flour, as well as thousands of gallons of milk for the homeless in San Francisco. Each bakery in town baked 2,000 extra loaves of bread; half was sent by rail to Oakland and San Francisco and the remainder was used for refugees who came pouring into Stockton. Schoolchildren took food to the supply boat that left the docks for San Francisco each afternoon. One man offered a cow a day as long as needed, and the Aurora Flour Mill donated 20 barrels of flour daily for the homeless in San Francisco.

Eight thousand dollars was immediately raised for relief and a number of local men went to the devastated city to help out. Two companies of the local National Guard were ordered to San Francisco. Households in Stockton were urged to share extra beds in their homes, and the Chamber of Commerce office became a clearing house for refugees. Refugee centers were established in the local halls, and church groups served meals. Everyone helped where they could, and Stockton once again became a magnet city, drawing people from San Francisco just as it had during the Gold Rush. City folks who had deridingly called Stockton "Mudville" suddenly found it a haven. A need had arisen and the people had responded, welcoming the homeless and providing a helping hand.

Stockton had escaped earthquake damage, but in

The Colberg fleet of small boats tied up to the head of the Stockton Channel serviced the isolated delta farming communities, carrying passengers, light freight, and mail. By 1928 Colberg received a government contract for delivering the mail, although until that time he had been providing the service for free. The stern-wheeler tied up alongside of the launches is the J.P. Peters. Courtesy, Stockton Chamber of Commerce

March of 1907 disaster struck in the form of a devastating flood. Most of the city went under water deeper than ever before. Some areas were under three feet of water as the Calaveras, Mormon Slough, and even the Stockton Channel overflowed. The city had been plagued with frequent flooding during the wet years of the 1850s, and even greater destruction occurred during the flood of 1862, which turned the Great Valley into a lake. This flood had so immobilized the city that no one could move about except in boats. Men wading through the streets in hip boots were apt to step into deep holes caused by raging water currents that made channels of the streets. After the water receded, the city lay covered in two to three inches of silt. Weber's beautiful garden on the Point was destroyed and never completely recovered. In 1871-1872 and 1889-1890 major floods again created havoc. In 1903, 1904, and 1906 parts of the city were under water again.

The root of Stockton's flooding problems lay at the juncture of the Calaveras River and Mormon Slough

Above: Relentlessly conscious of strikes and labor conflicts in the early years of the century, small Stockton businesses continued to give personal service. Here an employee of the American Fish and Oyster Company makes a home delivery to the Volpi house on Washington Street. Courtesy, M.A. Lawrence Collection

Right: Aside from the many people working on farms, in industrial plants, and local businesses, Stockton also had the independent tradesman. Here a Hunter Street vendor waits patiently at his wagon for customers needing their knives and tools sharpened. The building in the background is the Masonic Temple. Courtesy, Pacific Center for Western Historical Studies, University of the Pacific

in an area 16 miles northeast of the city at Bellota. Mormon Slough had at one time originated in the foothills three miles south of the Calaveras at Bellota. The Calaveras had created an alluvial fan that acted as a natural earth dam and diverted the stream in a sharp turn at that point. Only at very high flood stage did the water spill over this natural barrier and into a series of normally "dry washes" that eventually led into Mormon Slough.

What had taken nature years to build, man managed to destroy in a short time. A few farmers, through a series of manipulations, had inadvertently managed to divert the Calaveras River flow into Mormon Slough. The slough was not big enough to carry the water so it overflowed its banks. As time

went on, silt began to block the slough's entrance into Stockton Channel and made the situation in Stockton worse. As early as 1902 a state senate committee recommended the construction of a diverting canal east of Stockton to take the water out of Mormon Slough and put it back into the Calaveras, but the federal government controlled the waterways and bureaucratic action was slow.

The massive destruction of the 1907 flood served to counteract the inertia of the bureaucrats, and by November of that year it was announced the right-of-way was finally secured for the planned Diverting

Canal. Work started at Bellota but in January of 1909 the city was again flooded while workers toiled on the Mormon Slough levees east of town. Rumors spread that men from the north side of the slough in Stockton planned to cut the south levee to protect themselves. The south-siders patrolled their levee with shovels and guns to prevent this dastardly deed from occurring, and the city split into factions. Whether the rumor was true or not, an unhealthy climate of distrust pervaded the city. Nonetheless, the Diverting Canal was completed in 1911.

In the early years of this century, the labor movement made strides in organizing the workers of the Stockton manufacturing center. There were strikes against Holt Manufacturing, Stockton Iron Works, and the Globe Foundry during 1903 and 1904. The M.M. & E. (Merchants, Manufacturers and Employees Association), the Millers and Warehousemen's Association, and Sperry Mills supported the management position. The Feed and Flour Packers joined the strikers. By the time the workers in the city finally went back to work there

Floods continued to plague Stockton well into the 20th century. This view of San Joaquin Street looking northward provides a good picture of the front and upstairs porch of the Columbia House at the northwest corner of the inter- *section. Also visible are wooden sidewalks, a flooded pedestrian footbridge, and citizens checking the depth of the water. Courtesy, Pacific Center for Western Historical Studies, University of the Pacific*

had been considerable damage done to labor-management relations in the community.

From 1905 to 1914 labor conflicts were marked by violence. Most labor stoppages had been initiated by the labor movement, but on July 8, 1914 blaring headlines greeted Stocktonians: "Merchants, Manufacturers and Employers Association declares for open shop in Stockton. Stockton Millmen told to go to work under open shop or get their pay." Non-union men were brought from San Francisco to replace the fired workers. Private guards escorted the men aboard the steamer into Stockton.

Before long the city was paralyzed as every union in

Top: Built in 1916 at
Harding Way and Pacific
Avenue, El Dorado School
continues to stand as an
example of Elizabethan Tudor
architecture. Although this
picture was taken during Girls'
Play Day, the boys watching
out the second floor windows
show that everyone could enjoy
the activities. Courtesy,
Stockton Chamber of
Commerce

Above: Although the San
Joaquin County Hospital and
Almshouse entrance may look
rather bleak, the hospital itself
is rich in history. The
establishment began at the
East Street (Wilson Way)
complex in 1856, and in 1892
all the buildings burned to the
ground, luckily without the
loss of a single life. The
hospital moved to the 400-acre
parcel in French Camp just
south of Stockton in 1895,
where the hospital remains
today. Courtesy, Glenn A.
Kennedy

town got involved when they refused to cross picket
lines and boycotted M.M. & E. Association members.
Irving Martin of the *Stockton Record* editorialized,
discussing the starvation and devastation being
wrought by the war in Europe. He continued, "here
in Stockton under smiling skies surrounded by
bountiful crops with plenty to spare for every man—
here we are destroying every relation that makes
individual happiness and community prosperity
possible." He pleaded for arbitration to settle the
city's problems, caused by 900 workers who refused
to work in open shops or who were locked out of
their jobs for refusing to cross picket lines. Martin
later gave testimony at a hearing before a Federal
Committee of Industrial Relations in San Francisco,
and, when asked his opinion of what was happening
in Stockton, gave this assessment:

*This situation in Stockton in my judgment is not only
union and non-union. It is far deeper and broader than
that. It is absolutely a class situation. It is absolutely the
employers and financiers on one side and those who work
on the other. The class lines are just as absolutely drawn as
anything can be. This is a fight of class against class.*

It was Christmas of 1914 before the strike was
settled, with both sides agreeing to go to a committee

for arbitration in the future. This did not end the labor disputes, but they were never quite as serious or violent again.

Despite Stockton's labor problems the city continued to grow at a rapid pace. If a person had taken a riverboat out of Stockton in 1900 and not returned for 30 years, he would have had difficulty in recognizing the city, for the skyline had completely changed—dramatic evidence of a dynamic era.

In 1902 the Stockton Savings and Loan Society (now Bank of Stockton) started a new trend when it announced plans for Stockton's first skyscraper. The building was completed in 1906 and still stands on the northeast corner of San Joaquin and Main streets. The following year city boosters thrilled to the announcement of a new elegant tourist hotel of "Spanish Renaissance" style, to be constructed on Weber's Hole, a former channel lot at the head of Stockton Slough between El Dorado and Hunter streets. The construction contract for the new Hotel Stockton was signed in 1908, and the project, largely funded by local investors, was completed and dedicated in 1910. The new hotel dominated the head of the channel, permanently changing the Stockton skyline. In 1910 the Hotel Stockton became the showplace of the valley, with a roof garden that gave a dramatic view of Mount Diablo, especially on warm summer evenings when the sun set as a fiery red ball. The city council, which had finally used up its free rent in the county courthouse, moved into the hotel's second floor annex. Ironically, the councilmen ended up as tenants in a building on the site Weber had offered them years before.

Five high-rise buildings were constructed in downtown Stockton between 1910 and 1917. The most prolific designer of commercial buildings in Stockton was the architectural firm of Glenn Allen and Charles H. Young. Either individually or collectively Allen and Young were responsible for the Clark, the Wolf, and three other hotels; major apartment projects; eight commercial structures; seven warehouses and garages; three lodge buildings; two grammar schools, including the Lottie Grunsky School, and the Municipal Baths and Civic Memorial Auditorium.

Above: New subdivisions developed within the city limits, and many of the homes were single-family dwellings. Here a family at one such dwelling is seen enjoying a respite in the late afternoon. Courtesy, M.A. Lawrence Collection

Facing page, top: As more county roads and city streets were paved, the automobile became Stockton's primary mode of transportation. A wealthy Chinese cannery owner even purchased a fleet of Model "T" trucks to transport both cannery workers and produce at the Althouse-Eagal Fordson Company on El Dorado

Street. Courtesy, Pacific Center for Western Historical Studies, University of the Pacific

Facing page, bottom: The Number 12 car ran on Main and El Dorado streets. By 1892 the Stockton Street Railroad Company switched from horse-drawn cars to 10-horsepower electric cars. These electric cars built in local industrial plants were fairly small in size and held a total of 28 passengers per car. Courtesy, San Joaquin County Historical Museum

Residential development was just as active as commercial development during this progressive period of Stockton's history. Subdivisions cropped up in every direction. The real estate firm of Otto Grunsky and F.J. "Joe" Dietrich sold property aggressively, advertising in a wide variety of publications as diverse as the U.S. Navy magazine and

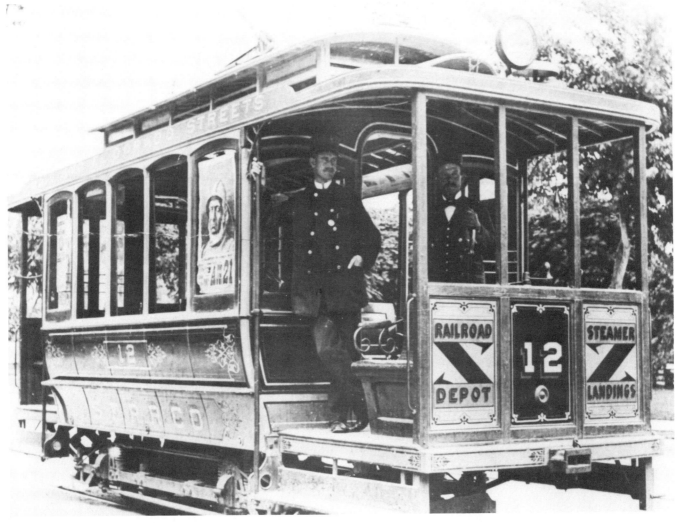

Italian newspapers. The firm sold property for as little as 1/48th down payment, "three dollars down and three dollars a month," according to one young realtor. The company developed several housing tracts including the Oaks, Brookside, Bours Park, Mossdale, Northcrest, Burkett Acres, and North, all in the immediate vicinity of Stockton. Before 1914 five more subdivisions were developed by others. In 1914 the city annexed North, Fair Oaks, and the Homestead area south of the city. The city was in the midst of a remarkable building boom that year and a Stockton reporter waxed with enthusiasm:

Think of it! Stockton ranked ahead of New York, San Francisco and all the other metropolitan centers of the United States, ahead of every city in the nation in building permits.

Transportation was a key to the changes wrought in the city of Stockton. By 1900 there were four electric streetcar lines that covered the city from north to south and east to west. By 1906 the system had doubled in size. In 1910 the streetcar lines were purchased by the Central California Traction Company, which ran 48 interurban trips a day in Stockton and north of the city to Sacramento. The Stockton Terminal and Eastern Railroad also offered service to the area northeast of the city to the farming community of Linden.

Public transportation encountered new competition, however, as improved city streets and county roads made automobiles more desirable. The city police department purchased a motorized ambulance and the fire department its first trucks in 1912. The police added a motorcycle in 1914, and the following year there were 1,152 automobiles in Stockton alone—not surprising, perhaps, in a city that had always been a transportation hub.

There was a great deal of entertainment available for the city during this time. There were traveling shows including Wild West shows and circuses, as well as local celebrations. There were stock company performances and Grand Opera. Appearances by as wide a variety of celebrities as prizefighters Jim Jeffries and John Sullivan, theatrical stars Ethel

The Hammond and Yardley Grocery Store, shown here in the 1910s, was one of the places patrons congregated in to exchange daily news. It was an ideal location, situated at 300 E. Weber Avenue, opposite the courthouse. Courtesy, Dohrman King

Barrymore, Al Jolson, Sarah Bernhardt, Marie Dressler, and Will Rogers were enjoyed by Stocktonians. In 1919 the County Fair was revived at Oak Park and was soon moved to the fairgrounds on Charter Way where a building was constructed in 1921. Horse races, automobile races, and demonstrations of that thrilling new invention, the aeroplane, took place on the fairgrounds.

Local movie fans flocked to the movie theater to see *The Whistle,* a William S. Hart film made in Stockton. In 1921 Stockton Radio pioneered as the Portable Wireless Telegraph Company (KWG Radio), which inaugurated a cooperative news service with the *Stockton Record.* Today KWG is the second oldest commercial station in California.

Stockton has always been a sports town with plenty of local participation. Baseball has always been popular. Babe Ruth played an exhibition game at Oak Park on October 23, 1924. Basketball was popular at the YMCA's new gymnasium. There was boxing, until the Women's Christian Temperance Union and churches got the city council to force boxing out of the city limits and into the county. Boys had always found places to swim in the sloughs and river but Yosemite Lake became the favorite spot in 1916. It was not only the place to swim but also the place to be seen. The Mineral Baths, which were eventually purchased by the city and became a public spa,

offered a full day of relaxation for the city's workers. Skating rinks had long been popular in town, and there were always dances, church socials, and school picnics to attend.

Saloons and houses of prostitution remained a part of the city, as they had been since Gold Rush days. Perhaps the most famous house was the "Bull Pen," constructed in Chinatown in 1905. It was located in the heart of the block; the actual spot can be seen today as the promenade called Chang Wah Lane located between Hunter and El Dorado streets. There was sporadic discussion of the vice in the local newspapers, but little was done until the state passed the Red Light Law in 1913. This provided a legal means for closing the Bull Pen and other such houses, but many prostitutes moved into at least one downtown hotel and the surrounding residential districts.

Liquor had become the target of a major anti-vice campaign at the turn of the century so prostitution continued under less scrutiny. Temperance leader Carry Nation and her vigorous campaign had not gone unnoticed, for children were being taught about the evils of "demon rum" in Stockton's schools and churches. The populace voted for Sunday closings of saloons but a second vote soon reopened them. When

The Anteros Club, a young bachelor club, performed many amateur plays between 1902 and the 1920s. Many important local names have been members and performers, such as Asa Clark, Dave Mathews, Henry Yost, Joe Gail, Warren Atherton, and Otto Sandman. Here the club members are enjoying a hayride on Sutter Street in 1905. Courtesy, Pacific Center for Western Historical Studies, University of the Pacific

California became the 29th state to ratify the 18th amendment speakeasies became as common in Stockton as in other parts of the country. There were reported to be as many as 23 illegal establishments in Stockton in an equal number of days after Prohibition went into effect. Home brew recipes were a dime a dozen and hundreds of homes became do-it-yourself breweries. G-men caught Stockton's share of moonshiners. As the city cracked down on illegal operations regular jitney services took patrons to the roadhouses out of town. Though Prohibition was a joke to some it was serious business to many who tried to enforce the law. Bad liquor had made some ill and killed others in town. Prohibition was no different in Stockton than in other places. Probably the greatest harm it did was give the average citizen a reason to break the law.

The community had been reminded about the war

Top: Two young men are depicted in this 1910 photo relaxing in the park in suits and derbies. The dress code was far more formal compared with today's standards. Courtesy, M.A. Lawrence Collection

Above: The Mineral Baths on South San Joaquin Street, first named Jackson Natural Gas Well Baths, were later named the McKinley Park and Pool. In the hot summers people flocked to the baths for a swim, a picnic under the trees, for band concerts, or to ride the scenic railway, making it the most popular place in the 1920s and 1930s. Courtesy, Pacific Center for Western Historical Studies, University of the Pacific

Above right: A local Stockton beauty, clad in her black silk dress and light color parasol, poses before the camera in 1905. Courtesy, M.A. Lawrence Collection

Facing page: Young boys dreaded church because they had to don their Sunday best. Here Roy A. Kennedy manages a half-hearted smile in spite of his clothes. Courtesy, Glenn A. Kennedy

in Europe during the labor strike in 1914 but that war was far away to most Stocktonians. The conflict in Mexico had much more impact, especially when the men of the Stockton Unit of the National Guard were the first troops sent to Nogales after Pancho Villa's raid. But the European conflict was more important to Stockton than most local people realized, as the Holt Brothers' Caterpillar attracted the attention of the military. The U.S. Army tested one of the machines by pulling an artillery piece through the mud; it proved equal to the job but unfortunately the army had no money to buy the equipment. Finally a British Army officer developed an idea for an armored vehicle, an idea he borrowed from a friend who had observed a Caterpillar at work. Eventually an eight-inch howitzer was added and the tank was born. As orders for the new equipment came in, great secrecy was placed around the Holt Brothers' plant. Soldiers guarded the entrances, and the public was told the vehicles were to be used as reservoirs to transport water to the British troops in Egypt. Reservoirs soon became "tanks" in the

vernacular of the Stockton workmen. When holes were cut in the sides of the tanks, the rumor spread that they were snowplows to be used in Russia; as camouflage, the words "with care to Petrograd" were painted on the side of each tank leaving the plant. In 1916 the truth was finally revealed when the *Stockton Independent* ran a story praising the performance of the British Armoured Motorcars.

Now comes word that these armoured motorcars are nothing more or less than the Holt Caterpillar, the product of a Stockton man's dream; little did he think when he produced his track laying tractor a few years ago to make possible the cultivation of lands too soft to be profitable when tilled by horses that his invention would be one of the world's greatest military assets.

On March 6, 1917 the country officially went to war against Germany. The announcement was followed, in Stockton, by an immediate effort to raise money with a Liberty Loan bond drive. With 2,400 workers at the Holt Manufacturing plant drawing an annual payroll of two and a half million dollars, there was little difficulty raising money for the war effort. Every bond drive exceeded expectations.

Selective service registration was instituted with 365 men designated as Stockton's quota. Before the local recruits left town a parade was held in their honor. Stockton became an assembly area for the draftees of several counties, and the Chamber of Commerce urged everyone to give the soldiers a rousing send-off; local girls gathered at the railroad depots to cheer the soldiers.

In October of 1918 as victory seemed imminent the city's population fluctuated between euphoria and depression as it looked forward to victory on one hand and fought the dreadful flu epidemic that hit the nation on the other. On October 16, 1918 there were 94 cases of flu reported in Stockton. Four deaths were reported the next day and within a week there were 1,170 cases in the city. An ordinance was passed requiring everyone to wear a mask. The flu epidemic raged from mid-October 1918 until the first of February 1919. All segments of the community were affected, but perhaps none worse than the Orientals who could not get into the hospitals. As a result, the local Japanese Association built the Nippon Hospital in 1920 to care for family and friends. The hospital only operated for a couple of years before the Japanese population became too sparse to support it.

When news of the armistice arrived in Stockton shortly after midnight on November 11, whistles blew and bells rang throughout the city. People jumped from their beds and headed for the center of town to celebrate. A parade was held during the day (with many of the participants wearing flu masks). Public and private celebrations went on for 24 hours.

The city basked in pride over its contribution to victory. Newspapers throughout the country heaped on praise for the Caterpillar tank. The *Chicago Tribune* wrote, "no single mechanical invention in the great war did more in a mechanical way to bring victory than did the machine designed for the uses of peace. The plowing engine metamorphosis became the Juggernaut." Another credited the tank with saving 20,000 lives on the Somme in the fall of 1916.

By war's end the Holt Manufacturing plant had

been completely converted for the production of tanks. Now the company had half-completed equipment and no market, for it had neglected the farm tractor market throughout the war years. The Best Tractor Company, founded by the son of the Best Company owner Holt Manufacturing had previously bought out, dominated the farm market. Benjamin Holt died in December of 1920. Financial problems plagued the company as some short-term notes came due. Finally, out-of-town financiers who had backed the Best Company proposed a merger that resulted in the formation of the Caterpillar Tractor Company. This proved to be Stockton's loss as Best management gained control and moved company headquarters to Peoria, Illinois, in 1925 to be closer to their markets. That same year the Sperry Flour Mill moved its operations to Vallejo. Thus Stockton lost two major employers in one year. Historian Glenn Kennedy wrote about the move of the two companies:

For years and years the local populace condemned Holt and Sperry as being "sweatshops" paying "coolie" wages and made many other undue assertions. They thought the town would be better off without them. The loyal workers of the two companies know better. At one time Holt had 4,000 employees. When both moved away, the local "wise-guys" woke up to realize how wrong they were. Stockton had lost something they could never have again.

In 1919 Santa Clara's College of the Pacific, the oldest private college in the state, began looking for a new home. Rumors were flying that the college would come to Stockton. By the end of the year two sites were offered and the school's trustees came to look them over. The school settled on a part of the Smith Tract, 40 acres of land traditionally used by the Italian gardeners. Classes were held in the Stockton Record Building with 40 students enrolled, as ground was broken in 1923. By 1924 there were nine buildings on the campus and by 1925, 605 students. The college has made a valuable contribution to the city's educational network.

During the World War I years building had slowed down; however, it was revitalized as Stockton entered a period of new growth and civic pride following the war. A city-wide reform movement was initiated, including a new zoning system developed to control the city growth. A new city charter, approved in 1922, provided for a city manager and that same year voters approved a million-dollar bond issue for public buildings. The city passed an ordinance outlawing the selling of farm products on city streets. The ordinance put the Italian Gardeners out of business overnight. Immediately the group appointed a committee to find a solution to its problem. The group organized the San Joaquin Marketing Association, but found that the Italian Gardener Society, being a non-profit corporation, could not own the association. Shares were sold and the group's leaders approached the

Machines always fascinated Ben Holt, as this photo attests. Here Holt (center) learns to master a flying machine after World War I, just prior to his *death in 1920. Courtesy, Pacific Center for Western Historical Studies, University of the Pacific*

Bank of Italy for financial support. According to local historian Tillio Boggiano, the bank's founder, Amadeo P. Giannini, said, "if it is for the farmers, yes!" They were granted the loan and built the association headquarters, known as Growers' Market, on the east side of Wilson Way near Weber Avenue. The growers continued to struggle until one of their members, Victorio Antonini, commenced hauling produce to San Francisco by truck. Soon Nathaniel A. Gotelli began trucking produce to Los Angeles and others followed. Thus the truck farmers of Stockton became major suppliers to two of California's largest cities.

The new city manager type of government went into effect in July 1923. Charles Ashburner was appointed city manager at a salary of $20,000 a year. He went to work immediately on city improvement projects, and received credit for the passing of another enormous bond issue in 1924. This issue included $1,500,000 for flood control—a dam on the upper Calaveras River at last! There was money for the Miner Avenue Subway, city parks, a new fire alarm system, street improvements, and new motor equipment.

Newly elected city officials enjoyed a honeymoon with the local populace. Local historian Glenn Kennedy wrote in 1967 of the usual treatment of politicians by Stockton's citizens:

Amusing as it may seem, each time new commissioners or councilmen were elected on election day they were the best that had ever been chosen. Six months later they were branded as not being any better than the last ones and it will probably be that way for as many years as the city elects new city fathers.

How true this was, for before long they nicknamed the new city manager "Cashburner," and the Miner Avenue Subway "Cashburner's Squirrel Hotel."

But those who wished to continue the improvement program pressed on. The Civic Memorial Auditorium was dedicated to the Stockton war dead in 1925, and the City Hall was added to the new Civic Center in 1927. More than nine square miles had been annexed to the city with the inclusion of residential areas as far north as the Calaveras River. Industrial development continued, and the Chamber of Commerce report recommended that the city encourage agricultural business.

In 1928 the population of Stockton was 56,000. There were 190 industries, employing 5,750 with an annual payroll of seven and a half million dollars. The value of industrial production was $38,000,000; the value of the previous year's county agricultural production was an impressive $52,000,000. The Stockton Chamber of Commerce Executive H.R. "Bob" Robertson coined the phrase "1,000 miles of waterways," as the city began to look back to its port to bring continued prosperity.

The roaring twenties had indeed been energetic years for Stockton, and the city looked forward to continued growth in the decade to come.

VI.

DEPRESSION, WAR, AND AFTERMATH

Stockton's economy remained healthy throughout the 1920s, up to and including 1929, despite ominous fluctuations in the stock market. After peaking in September the market plunged into a period of decline, followed by intermittent rallies until October when the crash toppled the nation's economy. Curiously, it is almost impossible to determine the actual date of the crash, or measure its national impact, by perusing local newspapers of the day, for business, at least in Stockton, went on as usual. The local economy received a boost when over two million dollars in privately funded building projects were pledged that year. Most important to the economic health of the city, however, was the deepening of Stockton Channel and the construction of the new port facilities, which were started in 1930.

The Calaveras flood control dam was completed in September of that year. Constructed as a shock absorber to take the pressure off Mormon Slough and the Calaveras River during periods of heavy storms, the dam promised to keep Stockton and the surrounding area from flooding. A dedication ceremony was held on November 2, 1930, during which City Manager Walter B. Hogan was praised for his efforts on behalf of the project.

On a cold, clear February morning in 1933, the S.S. *Daisy Gray*, the first ocean vessel to sail up the new deep-water channel, arrived in the Port of Stockton. Whistles blew and church bells rang, just as in the old days when a steamship would unexpectedly arrive in port. Approximately 1,000 people rushed to the dock to see the historical event. The ship, which carried 7,000 board feet of lumber, was efficiently unloaded as spectators watched from the dock. A formal celebration was held in the Civic Auditorium on April 5, 1933. The town welcomed special guests including California's governor, James Rolph, Jr.

The celebration marked the end of the long struggle that culminated in the completion of the dam project. The town had taken the first steps toward digging a channel to the sea in 1871, but the price tag proved too high to make the project a reality. In 1906 the Stockton Chamber of Commerce hosted the chairman of the National Rivers and Harbors Commission on a tour of the San Joaquin River to discuss the project again. He commented, "You ought to have 15 feet of water to the sea." That became the slogan until 1917 when, as ships became bigger, the slogan was changed to "17 feet to the sea." The Army Corps of Engineers held a local hearing and sent a report to Washington, D.C., in an attempt to get federal approval and funding for the project, but the First World War delayed all action. The Chamber of Commerce did not give up. It requested another hearing on the project, and in June 1919 a local delegation went to Washington and came home with authorization for a complete survey and cost estimate. After another local hearing, in which the Board of Engineers for Rivers and Harbors vetoed the project, the Chamber once again requested a hearing in Washington. It was August of 1924 before they brought home a recommendation to undertake the project. The following year city voters approved a $1,307,500 bond issue for the city's share of the project by a margin of 13 to 1. By January of 1926 both the House and Senate had approved the project

---

At the peak of the 1920s the city economy was thriving. Members of the Chamber of Commerce took an excursion on the J.D. Peters *to appreciate the wealth generated from the delta farms along the 1,000-mile long waterway. By then the 880-ton vessel had stopped its routine overnight run to San Francisco and was used only for excursion trips. Courtesy, Stockton Chamber of Commerce*

As automobiles became a common sight all over town, accidents unfortunately increased. The collision between these two cars on the corner of El Dorado and

Harding Way was nearly fatal to one of the drivers. Courtesy, Pacific Center for Western Historical Studies, University of the Pacific

and included it in a federal bill which President Calvin Coolidge signed on January 21, 1927. By this time the designated depth was at 26 feet. The right of way, land for the port, and land on which to deposit the excess dredged material was acquired. Work started in 1930 and three years later the *Daisy Gray* sailed into port.

In 1932 city voters approved a plan to establish a port district and Col. Benjamin Casey Allin, a former Houston port director, was hired to take charge of operations. The port authority, with the assistance of the Chamber of Commerce, convinced the Interstate Commerce Commission to approve the construction of a belt line railroad system that would offer equal access to the town's three transcontinental railroads. The Southern Pacific, the Santa Fe, and the Western Pacific railroads agreed to take turns operating the road. Before the channel project was completed another application was sent to Washington to deepen the channel to 30 feet. Approval came in 1935 and the second dredging was completed by 1940.

The port building project had a strong influence on the city's economic well-being, even though it did not show a profit until 1936-1937. Historian Nicholas P. Hardman estimated that the project, which employed over 500 workers, cut the local unemployment rate by 20 to 25 percent.

Stockton's middle class did not fare badly during the Depression years, although there were changes in the lifestyles of its citizens; courtships lasted longer as couples delayed marriages for lack of money to set up housekeeping. Stockton families who needed money could always earn a little extra in nearby farmers' fields, and women went to work in the drying yards, packing sheds, and canneries.

One area of Stockton that grew rapidly during the Depression years was the west end, called Skid Road. (The term was later corrupted to Skid Row.) It was the oldest part of town, encompassing Chinatown and the area west of El Dorado Street. Before the automobile became commonplace most farm workers had been housed on the farms, and came to town only when they were between jobs or to buy necessities. The old buildings of the west end had

Downtown Stockton boasted many restaurants and lunch counters where a good meal could be had for as little as 35 cents. The Park Restaurant, shown in this 1935 photograph, was later known as the P. K. Lunch, and had an international staff of waitresses, cooks, waiters, and

dishwashers. Also in the Main Street area was the Hart's Cafeteria and the Coney Island Chili Parlor, the local gathering place for the Greek colony in the 1920s. Courtesy, Pacific Center for Western Historical Studies, University of the Pacific

The Wool Grower's Hotel stands as one of the many places various ethnic groups sought for a sense of nativity. Built in the 1880s, the hotel served as the early center for Basque gatherings and feasts.

Other citizens of the city treated themselves to the distinctive and tempting Basque food available there. Courtesy, Stockton Chamber of Commerce

traditionally served as rooming houses for these seasonal workers. During the late 1920s and early 1930s Filipinos comprised the major farm labor force on the delta. The men gathered in town on weekends after a week of labor in the fields. Many of these men had gone from the Philippines to work in the fields of Hawaii and had come to the mainland looking for work when their contracts expired. Since the Phillipine Islands were under U.S. jurisdiction there were no quotas on immigration. Some of the Filipinos worked in the Imperial Valley in the winter and Stockton in the summer. Filipino-run businesses were opened to meet their needs and part of Stockton's west end was given a new nickname, "Little Manila."

The Filipinos were welcomed in the west end but not in other parts of the city, for some downtown hotels even posted signs that read, "No Filipinos." Eventually the city would have the highest Filipino population in the U.S. A second wave of Filipinos arrived after World War II. Many were former servicemen, more educated than the first group, and perhaps faced less prejudice because of this.

The Depression brought a large influx of migrants looking for jobs. Stockton's reputation for providing

The Great Depression brought another and more lasting problem to the city, the need for low-cost housing, which unfortunately created the climate for urban blight. Throughout the city's history its administrators had enforced strict building codes, but during the 1930s county officials allowed and encouraged subdivision with a minimum of required improvements. Often a graded street was all that was needed to start a development, and substandard housing on the edge of the city flourished.

Although Stockton's farmers did not go hungry they did not escape the Depression unscathed. They had difficulty paying their bills and in turn Stockton businesses suffered. The business community had always suffered periodic declines by extending credit to local farmers. The farmer had to wait until his crops were harvested to be paid, and expected the businessman to do the same. When agriculture shut down during the winter months, so did the business economy in town. But by 1940 the area had weathered the worst of the Depression and economic

Women moved into cannery positions as soon as the plants were opened. Adept and skillful, these women proved to be the essential unit behind the success of many local canneries. Here women are seen processing and canning asparagus at the Flotill Cannery. Courtesy, Stockton Chamber of Commerce

Stockton canning industries prepared for the heavy war demands as this Flotill cannery poster incited both patriotism and independence in women. It was one of the rare industries which guaranteed women a job after the war. Courtesy, Stockton Public Library

farm jobs turned Skid Row into one street-long hiring hall. Displaced farmers of the Midwest and the dust bowl were attracted to Stockton's farm jobs, especially in the disastrous year of 1934. They came from Oklahoma, Arkansas, Missouri, and Texas. Many settled in East Stockton, which soon became known as "Okieville." Most were farmers but a few opened small businesses.

Many of the city's laborers found employment through the W.P.A. (Works Progress Administration), which had come to the city and taken on various public building projects. Most young men were able to find jobs, for a strong back seemed to be the major criteria for employment at the time. But as the Depression deepened those over 40 had great difficulty finding jobs, and for those over 50 it was almost impossible.

prospects looked hopeful as the minimum wage went to 50 cents per hour for men and 37.5 cents per hour for women. As war hovered over Europe, lightning struck out of the west. On December 7, 1941, the Japanese attacked Pearl Harbor and every person in the city of Stockton would find his life changed. The following day San Francisco radio stations went off the air as that city, along with Los Angeles and Sacramento, underwent blackouts because of a report that enemy aircraft were within 21 miles of the California coast. On December 9 aircraft were again reported, this time just 10 miles off the coast, and Stockton too considered blackouts, although they never came to pass.

The disaster at Pearl Harbor took its toll among local Japanese as old animosities surfaced. Air raid warnings and radio blackouts frayed nerves as rumors spread that the Japanese intended to invade and occupy California to take the farmland they coveted. Talk of internment of the Japanese population increased as a belief spread that there were spies in the Japanese community whose purpose was to aid in the invasion. Sheer hysteria led to wild rumors that flew about the countryside. There were so-called

"strange lights" supposedly sending signals from prime targets in California, and there were reports of unusual ground signs sighted from the air.

All Japanese were now branded as "Japs" by most of the local populace, even the Nisei (those born in the United States). By spring the federal government ordered all Japanese to relocation centers. Families sold their belongings for next to nothing or packed them into boxes and stored them in any convenient location. Some used barns for storage or boarded up houses, which were soon looted.

The War Relocation Authority leased the county fairgrounds as a holding center for the local Japanese. The fairgrounds' horse stables were converted into dormitories. By May 1942, there were 490 Stockton High School students at the camp. High school teacher Elizabeth Humbarger, sponsor for the school's

A 1944 day-care center was three decades ahead of the licensed nurseries prevalent in the late 1970s. Following through with their ads attracting female workers that guaranteed continual employment after the war, Flotill Canneries also relieved working mothers' worries by providing a child care nursery on the cannery grounds. Courtesy, Stockton Public Library

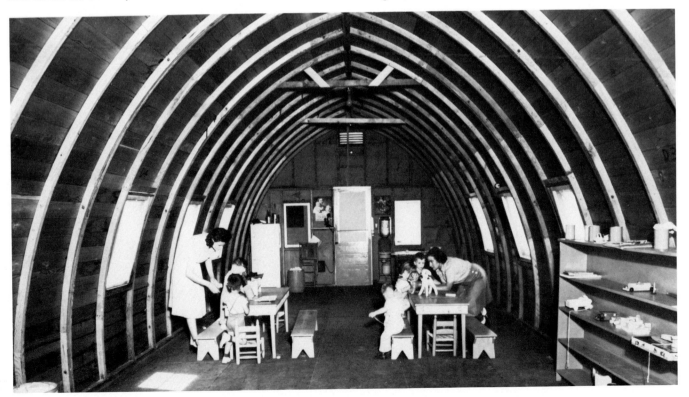

Left: During the war years Stockton boat builders numbered eight companies operating 10 shipyards with 10,000 workers. Among the large shipbuilders were Colberg, Stephen Brothers, Hickenbotham, and Pollick Shipyard, which was the largest, employing about 5,000 people. Here the Colberg Boat Works launches the USS ATR 52. Courtesy, Stockton Chamber of Commerce

Above: This photograph features a view of the Stockton Channel in the late 1930s, prior to the building of the Stockton grain elevators. Large ocean vessels found their way into the 26-foot-deep Stockton Channel as early as 1933 and by 1940 the channel was deepened to 30 feet. Clearly visible in the waterway is the turning basin. Courtesy, Stockton Chamber of Commerce

Japanese American Club, got permission to hold class at the camp for two hours per day. Acting as liaison, Humbarger asked the other teachers to send assignments to the students, enabling them to complete their school year. Most agreed. Humbarger organized the temporary school, enlisting college students to supervise the high school students. The plan worked; 92% of the students completed the year's work, and all of the senior class students graduated.

In October 1942 all of the local Japanese, including the Nisei, were sent to Rohor, Arkansas. Many of the young Nisei enlisted in the armed forces and served honorably during the war. In retrospect it is evident that a great injustice was done, the result of 50 years of prejudice and newspaper criticism of the Japanese in California. One might wonder if the city of Stockton, tolerant of foreign populations in the past, might have been so again had it not been for the spreading panic among the coastal cities.

During World War I, Stockton's Holt Manufacturing had made a significant contribution to the war effort with its tanks. But during World War II the manufacturing sector of the entire city launched into wartime production. In the shipyards alone the industrial work force grew from 2,500 in 1939 to 10,000 at the height of the war. Eight companies operated ten yards which built floating dry-dock sections, net tenders, rescue boats, submarine patrol boats, landing craft, transport ships, and small craft. Stockton companies received government contracts because they met the War Department's requirement that manufacturing of strategic military materiel be produced 60 miles or more from the sea in order to be outside the range of naval gunfire.

During the war years everything from aerial bombs and airplane parts to the reconditioning of army trucks and motors occupied the civilian work force, but it was the military installations that really changed the city. Most of the Port of Stockton, along with additional acreage, became the Stockton subdepot of the Benicia Arsenal, and was under army jurisdiction. Rough and Ready Island became the Naval Supply Annex, where the navy built the world's largest continuous concrete wharf to berth 13 ships in a single line. The army facility at Lathrop added to the city's store of military supplies and Stockton became the supply base of the Pacific. The local airport became an Air Force flight training school known as Stockton Field. It is no wonder that by the end of the war Stockton was considered the number one military target in California in case of enemy attack.

The city's population swelled during the war years, and emergency housing and military barracks were thrown up in and around the city. Downtown Stockton was bursting at the seams and the adjacent Skid Row grew.

During the World War II era another large

This picture of the southwest corner of California and Main streets depicts women during World War II. A U.S. Marine Corps recruitment poster on the sidewalk encourages women to enlist, while the WAC waiting at the corner is an example of the great number of women who did answer the call to serve their country. Courtesy, Pacific Center for Western Historical Studies, University of the Pacific

minority group appeared on the Stockton scene. There had long been a stable black community in Stockton, for some had come during the Gold Rush. There were black churches very early in Stockton's history and a black school had been established during the Civil War. After the children were integrated into the public school system there is little record of change in the black community, until the Second World War. Black military personnel were stationed in Stockton and the war brides of these servicemen followed. Others were attracted by the wartime industrialization of the area. Some of these new residents were Southern blacks with new-found freedom, who would never return to their former homes. Most settled in south Stockton in temporary government housing or in low-cost housing in the east part of town, some of which is still in use today. After the war some of the black servicemen returned to

Stockton to become part of the civilian government work force at the remaining military supply bases. The black community grew and suffered some discrimination, much of it caused by poor housing, leading to segregation in the schools. This created a new problem, which would have to be dealt with in later years.

Throughout the war years the area's agricultural sector suffered a severe labor shortage as former farm workers moved into wartime jobs. Field labor became scarce and fruit-pickers became almost nonexistent. High school students were encouraged to help harvest the crops and although schools were closed to facilitate their efforts some of the more perishable fruits were lost. Inmates from a German prisoner of war camp established at the fairgrounds also worked in the fields.

But these efforts to provide farm labor were not

An important military site during World War II, the Stockton Channel and the Stockton Naval Supply Depot on Rough and Ready Island (right) served as home for many naval ships after the war. This aerial view provides an excellent look at the ships of the Pacific Reserve Fleet tied up at the 6,500-foot-long continuous concrete wharf. Courtesy, Stockton Chamber of Commerce

Because of housing shortages during World War II, military barracks and emergency housing literally appeared overnight throughout the city. Building began with temporary trailers which within two months gave way to solidly constructed housing units. River View, southeast of the Port of Stockton, was constructed at the same time as Edison Villa and Parkside. Courtesy, Pacific Center for Western Historical Studies, University of the Pacific

enough as farmers were urged to produce more for the war effort. There was still a need for a more abundant labor force, so the Bracero Program was initiated to answer the need. Braceros were Mexican laborers brought into the area to work on the farms and in the orchards. Special camps were established as trainloads of workers arrived from Mexico. The Braceros were willing workers, earning American dollars to take or send home, and there is no doubt that they helped save California agriculture.

Although Mexican farm workers had been immigrating into the U.S. since the 1930s, few worked in the fields around Stockton, the exception being the sheep-shearers and livestock workers who had been part of Stockton's agricultural tradition since its early days. The Bracero program continued long after the war, and by 1964, when the program was finally shut down, more than half of the delta work force was made up of Mexicans. Many of these workers returned to Stockton under the new green card program or illegally entered the state to work in the fields, and Stockton's resident Mexican population grew.

After the war the military repair shops converted back to manufacturing farm machinery and trailers. Shipbuilders returned to making fishing boats, river

The first Bracero Program was instituted when the city fathers welcomed the arrival of Mexican nationals on June 18, 1943. For more than 20 years the program provided the work force in the San Joaquin area needed to sustain the tomato and asparagus industries. Courtesy, Stockton Public Library

barges, gold dredgers, luxury pleasure craft, and farm machinery. The Port of Stockton had been forced to neglect regular shipping during the war years, and found itself outside the mainstream of the shipping business. Bulk storage facilities for oil, iron ore, and liquids such as wine and molasses were added. New warehouses were constructed and became a major factor in the port's business. But increase in ship sizes and the depth limitation in the channel kept the port from competing with the coastal ports in the newly developing business of container shipping. Once again there was a move to deepen the channel, but once again it would take years to get through the red tape, and it would not be until the 1970s that the port began to show a healthy profit again.

Fortunately for the city the military bases did not shut down entirely. More than 6,000 civilian employees were hired at the Stockton Ordnance Depot, the Stockton General Depot (now Sharp's

Army Depot), and the Naval Depot, which became headquarters of the 19th U.S. Fleet.

Recovery from the pressures of a wartime economy was slow, but it did occur. Stockton now had time to turn to solving some of the city's problems. SUSD (Stockton Unified School District) was under great stress from the increase in population and school enrollment. Half-day sessions and overcrowded classrooms had unfortunately become the norm, so the school district instituted, in 1948, a so-called "6-4-4 system" to relieve the situation. The system allowed for six elementary grades, while the seventh through tenth grades were moved to the old Stockton High School on the corner of Harding Way and California streets. Grades 11 and 12 were included with the two years of Stockton College. The district had operated under the original grammar school/high school system for 82 years with no change until 1935, when the first junior college was organized, after two aborted attempts had been made in 1917 and 1921. The school district contracted with the College of the Pacific to operate Stockton Junior College under a rental agreement. The junior college facilities operated under this system until the new system was organized in 1948. The district renamed the facility Stockton College and moved to property just south of the Pacific campus.

After a series of successful bond issues and an expanded building program, SUSD changed the whole system again in 1952, this time to the 6-3-3 system, which allowed for six elementary grades,

Growth and permanence of the Sharpe General Depot at Lathrop added greatly to Stockton's population and economy. This picture shows dedication ceremonies of the

Sharpe Army Airfield and features the John J. Pershing hangar in 1960. Courtesy, United States Army Photograph

three junior high school grades, and three senior high school grades. There were now three high schools—Edison, Franklin, and the newly organized Stagg High School, which operated on the Stockton College campus until a new facility was opened in 1958.

In 1963 SUSD terminated the junior college program when San Joaquin Delta College was organized to serve a wider area than just Stockton. After considerable negotiations the new college district leased the old Stockton College campus and remained there until moving to the new campus on the former State Hospital Farm on Pacific Avenue.

Downtown Stockton encountered new problems in the postwar era brought on particularly by the increased number of automobiles. Parking became impossible and, giving in to frustration, people double-parked. The congestion caused frequent accidents; at times there seemed to be an accident at every corner. Skid Row continued to be the hiring hall for farm labor contractors who now found enough Mexican workers to meet their needs. Stockton had the dubious honor of having the largest Skid Row in the United States. The police department was factionalized, demoralized, and riddled with graft. Most of Stockton's police chiefs had been easy-going, good-natured men whose priorities were not discipline and efficiency.

In January of 1946 City Manager Walter Hogan appointed Rex Parker, a detective in the department, as chief of police, and gave him the task of shaping up the department. Parker, an energetic and apparently incorruptible man, set to work. He cleaned up the police station by making it a place of business instead of a local hangout for those who had nothing to do.

Some of the officers were reported to be on the take, accepting everything from a carton of cigarettes to large-denomination bills, so Parker decided to dry up the source of the money. Believing a local bookmaker to be the source of much of this graft money, he closed the business in March of 1946. He also made administrative changes and started training programs and a police reserve department.

In the spring of 1947 City Manager Hogan attended a conference on organized crime held by Governor Earl Warren. He returned home convinced that outside racketeers were moving into the old Stockton gambling community. He consulted with Parker, who immediately closed down the 16 wide-open gambling operations in town. Soon the Stockton employment office received applications and granted unemployment insurance checks to 400 self-professed professional gamblers.

Parker next went after the slot machine business and informed the owners of these devices that no money payoffs would be allowed, and that the machines could be used for amusement only. In taking these steps, Parker was stepping on previously untouched toes, for many of the local lodge halls used slot machine money to stay solvent. He also put the heat on local houses of prostitution, with the result that some of the girls left town or turned to working the local streets and bars.

In January of 1948 five new council members took office. One of them was a Skid Row businessman who would soon surface as the majority leader. Several months after taking office he invited the council members to his home for the evening. Most of them went, and admittedly, they discussed government business. The next day rumors spread that they would

ask Hogan to remove Parker from office. Some concerned citizens feared this meant that Stockton would go back to being an "open" town and made plans to resist the movement. But Mayor Jerry Keithley announced that the council would continue to support strict law enforcement. Things remained the same until August when Keithley resigned from the council to take a city job. A friend of the Skid Row businessman/councilman was appointed to the council in his place.

Before long the council pressured Hogan to investigate reports that Parker could not get along with his subordinates and implied that Hogan's job was at stake. Rumors spread again, and petitions were circulated by concerned citizens. One petition in support of Hogan and Parker contained 3,662 signatures. Another, carrying 80 policemen's signatures, declared there was a lack of confidence in Parker and a reluctance to serve under the chief.

The council could not fire Parker, but it could, and did, fire Hogan, and appointed his assistant Russell McGee as acting city manager. This was almost sacreligious in the minds of some, as Hogan had served the city faithfully for 28 years. A citizen's committee was organized. The Grand Jury met and recommended that Hogan be reinstated. When the council refused, the citizen group started collecting signatures for a recall of the six councilmen. The Stockton Record and a leading Stockton banker supported the recall. The opposition believed it could not get fair coverage in the newspaper. They retaliated by publishing their own newspaper, which was delivered to 25,000 citizens every ten days.

As the issues became more clearly defined, Stockton's citizens divided into two distinct camps. The pro-recallers were perceived by the opposition as rich, intellectual, and Protestant—all in the same group. This brought labor, the "common" man, and Italians, because most were Catholic, into the anti-recall camp. The business community tried to remain neutral, although there were some who believed an open town was good for business and others who had never forgiven Parker for closing down the slot machines at their clubs. The town's newer residents, who felt no particular loyalty to Hogan, leaned

toward the anti-recall movement. Others believed that since the policemen signed the petition against Chief Parker there must be some truth to the complaints about his leadership. Some members of the Stockton legal community muddied the waters further by offering unauthorized deals on both sides.

On election day 20,000 voters, more than in any previous election, turned out and defeated the recall by 1,200 votes. Local citizens shrugged their shoulders and went back to business as usual, but out-of-town newspapers headlined, "Stockton Voted An Open Town." One unbiased report was filed by Gordon Pate of the *San Francisco Chronicle*. He drew some interesting conclusions:

So far as opening the town goes, first, the Council is on record as opposing it, and second even if it wished to, it could not open the town at present. Too many people are watching, including the only newspaper in town.

The recallers had not really lost because the city never became wide open again. They had achieved their purpose. Hogan quietly retired but soon became a water consultant for the county, two water districts, and the Port of Stockton. After the new city councilmen took office the Calaveras Dam was renamed Hogan Dam in his honor. In 1959 he received special citations from the Army Corps of Engineers and the Secretary of the Army for his service in solving the area's water problems.

Despite the fact that the citizens of Stockton had become divided over the 1949 recall issue, there was one area of Stockton life that united everyone: that was football fever. Amos Alonzo Stagg, the Grand Old Man of Football from the University of Chicago, moved to the College of the Pacific well past retirement age for most men in the late 1930s and put together many winning teams. The Football Coaches'

As a result of the Christmas flood in 1955, a protest petition with 2,072 signatures pressed the Stockton City Council for an increase in the size of the Hogan Dam, built in 1930. The enlarged Hogan Dam, built by the U.S. Army Corps of Engineers, was dedicated in November 1960. Courtesy, Stockton Chamber of Commerce

Association awarded Stagg Coach of the Year honors in 1943. Stagg retired in 1946 and was replaced by coach Larry Semmering who put together another winner in 1949, the highest scoring team in the nation. The team played small colleges, so it did not receive national recognition, even though it scored a season total of 575 points. Semmering's team was undefeated and untied, yet uninvited to a bowl game. The team was headed by an unusually small quarterback, Eddie Le Baron, a master ball-handler who became a professional football star.

The year 1949 also saw the metropolitan area extend its boundaries as the county planning commission allowed a new development in the virgin area north of Stockton. Long-time Stockton realtor Greenlaw Grupe broke ground for the residential development of Lincoln Village in 1949 and the Lincoln Village Shopping Center in 1951. The district's one-room schoolhouse became the seed of a major new district, the Lincoln Unified School District. Unlike some other county developers, Grupe provided residents with adequate water and sewer facilities. The area was annexed to the city by degrees between 1955 and 1969.

Stockton city limits moved north of the Calaveras River for the first time in 1952. Several more parcels of land were annexed in 1954 and 1955. Charles M. Weber III started the Weberstown residential development along Pacific Avenue in the latter year.

Other developers followed, and housing complexes sprung up north of the river like mushrooms in the fertile soil.

Following the growth of the residential area north of the river, shopping centers were the next natural step in development. Weber developed the Weberstown Mall, one of the first covered shopping centers in California. Unfortunately, shopping malls proved to be bad investments for many during the 1960s because of the large sums tied up in buildings and the slow return. Weber fared no better than many when he lost his investment, in spite of the fact that he attracted major department stores like Sears and Roebuck and Weinstocks.

As the city moved north, less attention was paid to the southern part of town. When it came time to build a new bridge over Mormon Slough city officials decided instead to install a large culvert. In December of 1955 six inches of rain fell in three days in Stockton and even more in the foothills to the east. The Diverting Canal could not hold the water, and it overflowed at the point where it connected to Mormon Slough; the latter once again became a river. The city was endangered as culverts restricted the water flow. Dynamite and draglines were used in an attempt to remove the obstructions in the slough but the water continued to rise. City officials decided to save downtown Stockton and threw up a sandbag dike on the north levee. South Stockton went under water. On Christmas Eve in 1955 more than 3,000 people were evacuated in the east and south edges of town. The city fathers had talked of the need for a new enlarged Hogan Dam on the Calaveras River, but nothing had been done. The citizens of South Stockton gathered 2,072 signatures on a petition which they presented to the council demanding action to prevent future flooding. By September 1956 plans for a new Hogan Dam were on the drawing boards. No doubt the flood had given impetus to the project. The new dam was completed in 1964.

Other city improvements followed. The question of a new courthouse arose in 1944 as county government offices had, by that time, spread out to five downtown locations and to a Hazelton Avenue complex. A newspaper editorial suggested that all offices be situated in one building near the courthouse. The county decided not to abandon the old Court House Square but to demolish the courthouse and rebuild on the site. The county purchased the Hotel Stockton to be used as an interim courthouse while the new one was under construction.

The grand old building was razed and even though it had been condemned 30 years before, it took considerable effort on the part of the wrecking ball to bring it down. Ground for the new building was broken in 1961, and on October 10, 1964 dedication ceremonies were held. The zinc statue of Justice had been removed from the old courthouse dome and was placed at the west entrance to the building.

Center Street was extended across Stockton Slough and the extension of McLeod Lake east of Center Street was filled. The legal problems of filling Stockton Channel again proved problematical because of Weber's will. Charles M. Weber III proposed the construction of a ten-story office building with adequate parking, but the project was never begun. Weber and the city settled for providing parking space only; thus the parking lot sits on stilts today over the official head of navigation on Stockton Channel.

In 1962, after suffering three defeats, a library bond issue in the amount of $1,740,000 received voter approval and the city proceeded with plans for a new city facility in the Civic Center. The Stockton Library had come a long way from the two second-floor rooms it occupied in 1880. In 1884 it moved to the Masonic Temple. Frank Stewart's $5,000 legacy to the institution in 1889 enabled the city to build a two-story brick structure on a Weber-donated lot. Two years later Dr. W.P. Hazelton, a former Stockton resident, donated $75,000, which was used to construct a granite and marble structure fronted by marble Grecian columns. When the new library was built in the Civic Center the Grecian columns were moved to the College of the Pacific campus.

The two 1962 civic building projects—the courthouse and the library—cost more than all the civic improvement projects of the 1920s combined. In 1960 it was reported that one third of a billion dollars in building projects were in the planning stages for the city and ajdacent areas.

In the summer of 1960 the Chamber of Commerce organized Captain Weber Days, which grew into a ten-day sports spectacular. In 1964 the event was reported to have been attended by over 200,000 persons who enjoyed 29 major sports events from polo to autocross racing in downtown Stockton. The official celebration was discontinued in 1980, but some events are still held, with no sign of diminishing interest.

It is not surprising that Stockton has become a sports town, particularly when one looks at the community's long history of athletic activities. Much of the enthusiasm began with President Theodore Roosevelt's interest in physical fitness. In 1913 the schools allowed children a half day off to march through the streets of Stockton carrying banners asking for playgrounds. The pleas were answered the following year with the organization of a city playground commission. Bert Swenson became the

director of the department in 1918 and earned the title "Dean of Recreation" during his 36 years of service. He supervised the acquisition and construction of the municipal camp at Silver Lake in Amador County, municipal golf courses, tennis courts, swimming pools, and other playground facilities.

During 1944 the cooperation of the schools led to an expanded playground program, but it was 1954 that saw the biggest change—the organization of a new Metropolitan Parks and Recreation Commission.

By 1965 the city was booming. It had become a desirable place in which to live, with new homes, new schools, new highways, recreational opportunities, and jobs for most. From 1950 to 1965 more building and growth had occurred in the city than in the previous 100 years.

This view looking west from the head of the Stockton Channel depicts the Stockton of today. Courtesy, Richard S Minnick, Sr.

BY AUGUSTUS KOCH.

STOCKTON IN 1850.

BIRDS EYE VIEW OF THE CITY OF STOCKTON 1870. SAN JOAQUIN COUNTY CALIFORNIA.

1 COURT HOUSE.
2 FEMALE INSANE ASYLUM.
3 MALE "
4 WASHINGTON SCHOOL.
5 LAFAYETTE "
6 FRANKLIN "
7 1st BAPTIST CHURCH.
8 EPISCOPAL "
9 JEWISH SYNAGOGUE.
10 NORTH METHODIST CHURCH.
11 SOUTH "
12 CUMBERLAND PRESBY

13 CHRISTIAN CHURCH.
14 PRESBYTERIAN "
15 GERMAN "
16 R. CATHOLIC "
17 CONGREGATIONAL "
18 COLORED "
19 "
20 YOSEMITE HOTEL.
21 WEBER HOUSE.
22 LAFAYETTE "
23 GRANT HOTEL.
24 STOCTON "

90

25 ODDFELLOW BUILD?
26 DRUIDS HALL.
27 THEATRE BUILD?
28 STOCKTON WATER WORKS.
29   GAS   "
30 R.R. PASSENGER DEPOT.
31   "   FREIGHT   "
32 STOCKTON LUMBER YARD.
33   "   CITY FLOUR MILLS.
34 LANES   "   "
35 EUREKA WARE HOUSE.
36 GLOBE IRON WORKS.

37 W? P. MILLERS CARRIAGE FACT?
38 CONDY BROS! SASH & BLIND FACTERY.
39 TURN HALL.
40 RACE TRACK.
41 M.L. ABRAMSKY, REAL ESTATE AGENT.
42 ELDORADO BREWERY.
43 CITY BREWERY.
44 STOCKTON IRON WORKS.
45 PACIFIC TANNERY.
46 YO SEMITE CLOTHING HOUSE.

This hand-colored lithograph, derived from the original painting by Augustus Koch, portrays a bustling, developing Stockton in the 1870s. Commercial boats and trains entering the town from the north and south took advantage of the inland port city. Courtesy, Amon Carter Museum

Left: This painting of a youthful Captain Charles M. Weber by local artist Oscar Galgiani hung in the north wing of the State Capitol for more than 30 years. It now adorns the council chamber in city hall. Galgiani painted Weber's face from an old daguerrotype, while the rest of the portrait contains symbols of Stockton and Weber's legacy. Courtesy, Richard S. Minnick, Sr.

Facing page, bottom left: This Greg Custodio mural in the foyer of city hall represents the community spirit of the early pioneers and the important contribution each made to the development of Stockton. Courtesy, Richard S. Minnick, Sr,

Facing page, bottom right: This brilliant seashell picture was one of many unusual promotional cards produced by the Holden Drug Store, which was founded in 1849 by Dr. Erastus S. Holden. His son Isaac sold the family business in 1892, and after several proprietors the store folded in the 1950s. Courtesy, M.A. Lawrence Collection

Greeting cards for special occasions became a fashionable method of advertising among many Stockton merchants. Rosenbaum and Crawford Clothiers sent this embossed Easter greeting to their many customers after the turn of the century. Collecting merchants' cards became a popular hobby during that time period. Courtesy, M.A. Lawrence Collection

Above: For 75 years this nine-room house belonging to the Karl Simon family graced the corner of Madison and Fremont streets. In 1980 the Lou Galli family bought the Queen Anne cottage and barged it through the deep-water channel around various riverbends to its new location north of Tracy. Courtesy, Betty Galli

Left: A hand-carved lion's head on a cherrywood mantle is one example of the elegance in Victorian homes. This mantle was made in 1895 for Karl and Louise Simon's house. Courtesy, Betty Galli

The Pioneer Room at the Haggin Museum contains an outstanding artifact collection that carefully documents Stockton's history. Courtesy, Haggin Museum

Above: The College of the Pacific changed its name to the University of the Pacific in 1960. Through the main gate is a view of Burns Tower, built in 1963. Named for its late president, Robert Burns, the tower houses administrative offices and a water tank. Photo by Bela Fischer

Left: The 165-acre San Joaquin Delta College campus is situated on the former State Hospital farm grounds. Located in the heart of town, the graceful setting of the two-year college lends itself to a blend of the Mother Lode influence and the Spanish mission era in California. Photo by Bela Fischer

Above: After the redevelopment program of the 1960s the area of Stockton's Chinatown hardly resembled the lights, sounds, and color of yesterday. City officials deemed it respectful to erect some landmark to designate the old settlement. Visitors pass under the Chung Wah Lane gate to stroll the block-long promenade, stepping over lucky dragons and Chinese symbols in the cut tile inlay. Courtesy, Stockton Chamber of Commerce

Above: Beautification of the downtown area in the 1960s included the closing of Main Street at Hunter Square and the creation of a fountain-centered plaza west of the San Joaquin County Court House. Courtesy, Stockton Chamber of Commerce

Right: This golden California bear guards the pillared Stockton Memorial Civic Auditorium. The cornerstone for the building was laid in November 1924, and the following year on Armistice Day, veteran units dedicated the 5,000-seat structure to Stockton's fallen sons. Photo by Bela Fischer

Left: A clear day and graceful trees surrounding sparkling water add beauty to a canoe outing in a local Stockton residential area. Photo by Bela Fischer

Facing page, bottom: Stocktonians' love for the delta waterway and the joy of living on waterfront property have inspired housing developers to build man-made lakes and inlets as part of the special features in their subdivisions. This intricate canal system in a modern apartment complex serves as an aesthetic urban version of the delta waterway. Courtesy, Stockton Chamber of Commerce

Below: Mammoth ocean-going vessels laden with cargo sail through the heavily-traveled deep-water channel. Sailing enthusiasts enjoy working their way up the Stockton Channel and look forward to participating in the many boat parades and regattas scheduled throughout the year. Courtesy, Stockton Chamber of Commerce

Facing page, top: After vacating their quarters in the San Joaquin County Court House, the Stockton city officials needed a building large enough to house their offices. The result was the city hall building constructed on El Dorado and Lindsey streets in 1926. Courtesy, Stockton Chamber of Commerce

Facing page, bottom: This sugar beet field on the outskirts of town lies among many acres of rich farmland in the great Central Valley. Stockton naturally became an agricultural center because of its proximity to the Stockton Port and surrounding farmlands. Courtesy, Stockton Chamber of Commerce

Left: Nothing is more peaceful and calm than sunrise on the San Joaquin River. Courtesy, Sandra Groves

Left: Founded by Italian immigrant Manlio Silva in 1926 and led by the celebrated Korean maestro Kyung-Soo Won for the past 17 seasons, the Stockton Symphony represents the pinnacle of Stockton's cultural influence. Historically, the symphony is the fifth-oldest continuous service orchestra in California. Courtesy, Steve Pereira

Above: A crowd of spectators witnessed the Majestic Explorer *on her maiden voyage at the Stockton Yacht Club. Photo by Bela Fischer*

Right: Sails filling with gentle wind, this sailboat leaves the head of the Stockton Channel, gliding past Stockton in the early morning light. Courtesy, Stockton Chamber of Commerce

Rounding the bend of the Calaveras River is one of the many tributaries leading to the San Joaquin River near the inland port of Stockton. This early morning delta scene is as typical today as it was at the founding of the town in the 1840s. Courtesy, Stockton Chamber of Commerce

VII.

THE METROPOLIS

Stockton changed from a settled community to a rapidly sprawling metropolis during the 1950s, bringing new urbanization problems and unrest to the 1960s and early 1970s—another pivotal period in the city's history.

As suburbs developed under county control around the city, community leaders became absorbed in the problems of decay in the 100-year-old inner city. In 1955 Mayor Dean De Carli appointed an Urban Blight Committee to study the city's problems. The first urban renewal project was undertaken in east Stockton in the vicinity of Myrtle Street and Highway 99. This was a slum area which had been originally developed under the county government in the late 1800s and which had deteriorated badly during the Great Depression. Wood and tarpaper shacks had grown like toadstools from lots as small as 25 by 50 feet. The district was cleared and rebuilding was begun. Low-income housing projects were developed under city regulations on a portion of the land. Two new schools, a steel company, and other building projects renewed the area. Room was saved for a highway interchange and for a crosstown freeway to connect with the proposed Westside Freeway (today's I-5). This same crosstown connection was still far from completion by the early 1980s.

In 1958 the city council organized the West-end Redevelopment Project, which proved to be a political football. The major conflict occurred over whether to completely or partially demolish a nine-block area containing 162 rundown buildings and 48 bars. This was the very heart of Stockton's infamous Skid Row. After much heated discussion and two votes by the city council the resolution to demolish the whole area was passed. Criticism was levied at the council by those opposing demolition but the council held steadfast. Condemnation proceedings on a few of the properties delayed the project until 1964. The following year the west end took on the appearance of a war zone as the wrecker's ball leveled block after block of Skid Row. Only three buildings were left in the nine-block area, the old Eureka Grain or Farmers Union Warehouse, the Nippon Hospital, and the Sperry Flour office.

The two major ethnic groups that had been strongly entrenched in Skid Row were given priority to rebuild. The Lee Family Association built on the south side of the old Chinatown block and other Chinese associations and individuals filled the remainder. Filipino community leaders replaced "Little Manila" with a block of retail stores, offices, and a high-rise apartment building. El Dorado Street became banker's row and Center Street on both sides of the channel became the site of two modern motels.

The downtown shopping district continued to deteriorate as shopping centers were developed close to the new bedroom communities in north Stockton. Early in the 1960s an attempt was made to improve the business district as new facades were constructed on existing buildings and one-way streets were established to improve traffic flow. The buildings on the west side of Hunter Square were refurbished and an extensive beautification project was undertaken. A mall was created by closing off the west end of Main Street and a striking new fountain was added to embellish the area. Throughout the downtown area

Nightfall adds beauty and dramatic effects to the Hilton Hotel and the grand canal at the Venetian Bridges shopping area. Photo by Bela Fischer

old buildings were condemned to make way for parking lots. But every time this was done more businesses closed, thus giving the general public fewer and fewer reasons to fight traffic to get to downtown establishments. To complicate matters even more, the demolishing of Skid Row left a void in low-income housing for the farm workers, indigent, and elderly, many of whom moved into the now aging and deteriorating downtown hotels.

The late 1960s were turbulent years for Stockton, as they were for many other cities. The first and only successful recall of a city councilman occurred in 1967. The previous year the city council had organized a charter revision committee to explore the possibilities of a mayoral system, and the public became uneasy. A city planning commissioner resigned in protest, accusing Councilman/Mayor James Rishwain of interference in a zoning matter. Next the city fired a deputy city manager and a citizen's group rose in protest, threatening to recall the full city council. By the following spring opposition to the mayoral system had swelled when the results of a private survey among local service

By closing off the west end of Main Street and adding a fountain, the Hunter Square Plaza no longer reminds oldtimers of the fairs and expositions held at that location in the past. However, historic buildings such as the Bank of Stockton, California Building, Grupe Building, and the Fox California Theater stand as solid remembrances of the city long ago. Courtesy, Sylvia Sun Minnick

clubs revealed there was an overwhelming desire to retain the city manager type of government. The matter was finally settled at the polls when Rishwain was recalled by a two-to-one vote. The local newspaper tried to calm the troubled waters.

The next major political issue arose in 1968 when minorities protested the method used to elect the city council. The city was divided into nine districts with a requirement that one councilman must reside in each district; however, the voting for each was held city-wide. When an individual representing a south Stockton district won an election but did not carry his own district, the district voters protested vehemently and the general population agreed. In November

1969, the city council voted 6-3 to put district voting on the ballot. The general public confirmed the decision and the system was changed to district voting, allowing only those in each district to vote for their representative.

In 1969 the city council was seeking a strong city manager who could deal with the politics and the urbanization problems of Stockton. They found the man they were looking for in Elder Gunter, a man described by many as a first-rate problem-solver. He brought with him 25 years of civic experience, including the management of six cities. Gunter faced major problems immediately. Perhaps the most serious was a cease-and-desist order clamped on the city by the state to prevent further industrial development because of inadequate sewer facilities. This was aimed directly at the food processing industry, which produced a huge volume of sewage during the peak of the canning season. And, there were other problems such as complaints of police brutality which culminated in a riot at an Oak Park rock concert on April 29, 1973. Urban renewal issues also loomed large. As the new city manager and city

There was still much open field between the Weberstown subdivision (left) and the Sherwood Manor estates (right) in the early 1960s. The field eventually became two shopping malls 10 years later.

The State Hospital farm complex on Pacific Avenue (center) was to give way to the modern campus of San Joaquin Delta College in 1972. Courtesy, Stockton Development Center

council faced inner city problems, there was an even larger problem to be dealt with by the SUSD (Stockton Unified School District) in solving the problem of school integration.

As Stockton moved north so did the city's affluent, which left the low-income population and minorities in south and east Stockton. Edison High School in the south end of town had a large percentage of minorities, principally blacks, Hispanics, and Orientals. Franklin High School on the east side of town had the most balanced racial mixture but it was predominantly low income. The major racial conflicts occurred on this campus. Stagg High School in the north became almost all white, analogous to the already white Lincoln Unified School District further

north. A busing plan was proposed by an integration committee, but strong opposition arose, delaying action. Minority groups protested integration delays and another class struggle took place in the city. Court action finally forced busing on the Stockton Unified School District. The district lost enrollment because of "white flight" into the north suburbs, which swelled enrollment in the Lincoln Unified School District. SUSD officials predicted a two-million-dollar deficit in 1972. The city grew so far north it stretched into the Lodi Unified School District, another predominantly white school system. The north end did not stay all white, however, as federal funds provided for some low-income housing and developers built many multiple-housing units to fill the area's need.

Morris Chapel was built in 1942 on the University of the Pacific grounds, and houses the Methodist Archives. Ivy gracing the exterior walls of the chapel, coupled with the rose bridal path, proved to be the favorite location for many students, alumni, and local citizens' weddings. Courtesy, Pacific Center for Western Historical Studies, University of the Pacific

By 1982 SUSD enrollment had started to rise again and predictions are that the trend will continue. The district continued to have financial and management problems, and in both 1981 and 1982 grand juries recommended that the school trustees resign and be replaced.

The northward population growth can also be attributed in part to the expansion of both the community college and the university. San Joaquin

Delta College moved to a new campus in 1972. After a long struggle over site selection, the district purchased the old State Hospital Farm on Pacific Avenue. Old buildings and a large number of mature trees occupied the site. The buildings were demolished but the trees were saved. A modern campus was constructed in an old environment, creating a unique setting. Today the college serves not only San Joaquin County but some areas of surrounding counties as well.

The College of the Pacific became known as the University of the Pacific in 1960, with the former becoming a liberal arts college within the university. The university consists of a number of colleges offering studies in liberal arts, music, engineering, education, pharmacy, and business/public administration. It offers off-campus study in foreign countries, the McGeorge School of Law in Sacramento, and the School of Dentistry in San Francisco. The university, which is a chartered Methodist college, is privately funded and is the oldest private institution on the West Coast. It adds considerably to the cultural richness and the economic health of the city of Stockton.

The new residential area in north Stockton moved west into the delta as Fritz Grupe, son of the Lincoln Village developer, built a planned community of mixed housing. This is Lincoln Village West, situated between Fourteen Mile and Five Mile Sloughs on land below sea level. Grupe took advantage of this unique situation, constructed a man-made lake and built homes, apartments, and condominiums on the shore. The company won national awards for its development, but Stockton reaped the most benefit because it led to a new trend in the city and focused attention on the water at the city's doorstep. Grupe continued to develop lakeside communities and other developers took up the waterfront theme.

Urban sprawl had long exceeded the bounds of Capt. Charles M. Weber's well-planned city of ample streets. Getting across town became more and more difficult with only two main north-south arteries, El Dorado and Pacific avenues, to carry the north-south flow of traffic. Construction in the north end of the city was spurred on with the completion of I-5 (Inter-

state Highway 5) through the city. Final completion of the last 15 miles of highway between Stockton and Sacramento took longer than planned because of the attitude of Governor Jerry Brown's administration toward building freeways. But the opening of the final leg of the freeway probably did more to improve the city's image than any other event in its history. There had always been beautiful homes on tree-shaded streets in town but travelers never saw them. They saw instead the slums along Highway 99 and the old rundown areas in south Stockton. At one time the famous Lincoln Highway cut right through the heart of Skid Row. For these reasons the city was considered a dirty town by many. When the I-5 bridge was constructed across Stockton Channel travelers were treated to a panoramic view of the city, including an impressive overview of the port.

The Port of Stockton experienced major problems during the early 1970s. A series of port directors were hired and fired, commissioners squabbled, and the facility lost money for seven years. There was talk of closing the operation down. A grand jury commissioned a study and action was taken to remedy the situation. The port commissioners hired a dynamic new port director, Alexander Krygsman. Krygsman managed to turn the situation around. Ships were still growing in size and the channel needed deepening again. The project had been approved in 1965 but was stalled in the red tape of environmental issues. Krygsman went to work and the project was reactivated. The Army Corps of Engineers let the contract in September of 1982 and dredging was begun in 1983. This time the goal was 38 feet to the sea.

In the 1850s Stockton's water table had been as high as 35 feet from the surface. Deep artesian wells were drilled and the excess water ran into the nearby sloughs. Householders did not look to the city to take care of their water needs as each had his own shallow well, water tank, and windmill. In Stockton, everyone was more concerned with excess water than the lack of it. City officials had been amused observers when, in the early 1900s, farmers from the Calaveras River and the Mormon Slough fought each other for irrigation water in the Linden/Bellota area

A 1,081-ton building module is shown here being moved from its construction site to a barge on the waterfront, its destination Prudhoe Bay on the north slope of Alaska. These modules, built in Stockton in 1983, are a part of the "waterflood system" to increase oil recovery while the "wellpad manifold system" is to maximize the use of SOHIO's 150 miles of crude oil flowlines. Courtesy, Richard S. Minnick

in eastern San Joaquin County. The San Joaquin East Water District (now Stockton East Water District) was organized to settle that battle but it was years before the city became concerned with the supply of drinking water. It was in the 1970s, when saline water began to show up in the wells on the west edge of the city, that concern began to grow. The city joined the San Joaquin East Water District and took up the fight for completion of the proposed Folsom South Canal down the east side of the Great Valley to bring American River water to the area.

Stockton's reliance on deep-water wells became critical as both urban and agricultural areas drew more and more water from under ground. The water table dropped dramatically and brackish water continued to intrude on the freshwater pool under Stockton. The water district joined with the city to pipe water from the Calaveras River at Bellota to a new water treatment plant on the east side of town in 1976. In spite of this, water conservation measures were necessary to maintain the water supply during the drought of the late 1970s. The Calaveras River, unlike many of the rivers that flow out of the Sierra Nevada range, does not drain a snow area thus

providing a year-round water flow; it has only rainwater runoff, which cuts down the water quality. The city applied for delta water, even though it was of questionable quality, but dropped the application in 1984 as the Stockton East Water District signed a contract for New Melones water from the Stanislaus watershed.

As the city tried to find solutions to its water problems, a rapidly expanding population created urban sprawl. By 1980 the population within the city limits had reached 149,779; another 55,610 residents living adjacent to the city limits increased the Stockton metropolitan population to 205,389. In 1983 the city population showed an increase of 17,912, raising the total number of metropolitan residents to over 220,000. Although there is some duplication of city/county services, city services are often strained by the burden of additional county residents. This condition continues to cause conflicting interests between city and county governing bodies.

The population continues to grow as new immigrants arrive in Stockton. It is now the Southeast Asians, Vietnamese, Laotians, and Cambodians who are struggling to make their place in the community. Despite efforts by some to stop the influx of refugees, Stockton will no doubt, as it has in the past, accept these minorities into the mainstream of the community.

Because the mechanization of agriculture has reduced farm labor needs, there is a need for more industrial jobs to provide employment for these new immigrants. It took the city eight years to solve the sewer problem that hampered the development of new industrial plants. A new sewer facility costing over $16,000,000 was installed in 1979, but industrial development does not come easily. A major waterfront industrial project created controversy in 1981 as land across the channel from the port was proposed for the site of a Sohio (Standard Oil of Ohio) project to consist of modular building units to house pumping facilities for the Prudhoe Bay Alaskan oilfields. The question was whether there should be industrial or residential development across the channel from the port. This time business and labor

An aerial view of the north-south main arteries of El Dorado and Center streets in the 1960s shows the park bounded by city hall, the public library, the Civic Auditorium, and a used car lot. Until 1947 McLeod Lake extended through the park area to El Dorado Street. In the background one can see the Stockton Channel and what is left of McLeod Lake. Courtesy, Pacific Center for Western Historical Studies, University of the Pacific

presented a united front before the city council in support of the industrial development and the project was approved. During 1982-1983 modular units were constructed on the site and transferred to barges for shipment to San Francisco Bay and Alaska.

The city promoted innovative solutions to urbanization problems during the 1970s. Both manpower and affirmative action programs were utilized to solve urban ailments. New sewer and water facilities, as well as new streets, met the city's physical needs. A waterfront sea wall and 15 new parks met aesthetic needs. The city continued to annex the bedroom communities to the north. Under the leadership of City Manager Elder Gunter, Stockton applied for and received a large share of federal funds. It was the first city in the nation to receive a Housing and Community Development Block grant. This amounted to $1,803,000, but was only a small

portion of the $82,000,000 in grant funds received during Gunter's seven years as city manager.

There has been a continuing attempt to revitalize downtown, both by the city and federal government. The federal government offered tax incentives to rehabilitate old buildings although, outside of a few newcomers in the community, residents did not launch into these projects until inflation changed the economics of remodeling. It suddenly became more cost-effective to rehabilitate an old downtown building than to build a new one in the north end of town. As refurbished offices became available the legal community moved back into the court-house area.

Grupe Development Company bought and completely remodeled the old high-rise bank building on the corner of Main and Sutter streets. The company used the building for a time, then sold to the State Savings and Loan Association. Soon the rapidly expanding financial institution was renting or buying and refurbishing old buildings all over the area. When the association merged with American Savings and Loan in 1983, downtown Stockton became the headquarters of the largest savings and loan in the nation.

Downtown Stockton had always been a government center, but it gradually became a financial center as well. Office workers flooded the inner city during the day but deserted it at 5 o'clock, returning home to residential areas outside the city. In 1981 an R/UDAT (Regional/Urban Design Assistance Team) study sponsored by the American Institute of Architects was conducted in Stockton. A team of experts swarmed over the inner city for a weekend and came up with an ambitious plan to revitalize the downtown area. The City Planning Commission began designing a completely new city plan along the lines suggested. The plan took two years to formulate and was released in 1983. In the meantime more buildings were being restored to their former beauty and were made functional for modern offices. Hope rose anew for the downtown area.

Politically the city still has its problems, just as it did in the past. Almost every city council in Stockton's history has been fair game for criticism. After all these years the council members are paid only $15 a meeting, but there has been a continuing movement by the business community to increase the pay. Would paying the city council members more money ensure better government? When Elder Gunter, former city manager, was asked that question, he addressed the real problem. "I have always supported better compensation for council members," said Gunter, "but I don't think pay by itself would solve the problem." "What we need is strong community support to back candidates. That would mean district voters should back candidates who look at the overall city as well as their districts." Gunter's answer puts the issue of good government right back where it belongs, in the voters' lap. Only time will tell if the city meets the challenge.

The city's fire department has moved eons from the days of the bucket brigades that dipped water from the Stockton channel. The department has had a class one insurance rating for years; at one time it was only one of five cities in the nation with that honor. A paramedic program has been added in recent years to supplement the city's excellent medical facilities. St. Joseph Hospital's emergency cardiac care and Dameron Hospital's burn unit are among the best. The city's police department has come a long way too, since the corruption of the 1940s.

The cultural life of Stockton is rich. There are 110 churches, which have always had a strong influence in the community, many of them helping to maintain the ethnic heritage of their parishioners. Fine music, dance, and live theater are continuing community programs. The city enjoys an excellent museum and art gallery, Pioneer Museum and Haggin Art Galleries, in Victory Park, and numerous private

Stocktonians saw the Rosenbaum & Crawford Building, built in 1880, razed in 1916. In its place they watched the construction of a granite and brick skyscraper known then as the Farmers & Merchants Bank. Little did architect George W. Kelham know that the building, now the California Building, would be listed on the National Register of Historic Places and is also Stockton Historic Landmark Number 25. Courtesy, Sylvia Sun Minnick

galleries throughout the city add to the cultural diversity. The Stockton City Arts Commission sponsors and encourages artistic endeavors, while the Stockton City Cultural Heritage Board deals with Stockton heritage and historic preservation under the City Planning Commission. This board has been responsible for saving many old Stockton buildings. The group also organized and created the Magnolia Historic District, an area of fine older homes west of California Street and south of Harding Way.

Numerous social and service clubs and lodges have been an integral part of the community throughout its history. Urbanization has not diminished sports participation. Youth groups and sports activities abound. In addition, there are 47 parks, 22 playgrounds, 16 theaters, 5 golf courses, an ice arena and skating rinks, 68 tennis courts, 3 stadiums, 2 large auditoriums, a sports center, and 29 softball diamonds.

Today Stockton Channel is once again crowded with vessels, this time with pleasure craft lining the shore. Marinas cluster around the city providing hundreds of boat berths. A cruise ship makes regularly scheduled seasonal trips through the delta to anchor in the Sunrise Port. The old grain warehouse on the waterfront has been converted into a shopping

Above: Within the Catholic cemetery on Harding Way, almost hidden from view by four overgrown juniper trees, the tomb of Charles M. Weber and his family stands as a strong but quiet reminder of the pioneering families who saw the fruition of their dreams in the growth and development of the city of Stockton. Courtesy, Sylvia Sun Minnick

Below: The enlarged Hogan Dam helped but did not halt floods, as this picture of a 1983 flood at Yosemite Lake attests. During that flood high tide reached 10 feet above sea level, reminding Stocktonians that nature's forces are greater than man's means to change the environment. Courtesy, Richard S. Minnick

mall with five restaurants and is the new home of the Greater Stockton Chamber of Commerce. The West-End Redevelopment project now includes luxury condominium office towers, senior citizen housing, and apartment complexes; plans are under way for single-family homes and waterfront condominiums. Stockton is changing and growing as it becomes increasingly urbanized.

The city has its problems, but problems are solved by people. Stockton's problems have often been county problems. The conflict between the city and county governments has always been there, but it is changing as the city grows and the metropolitan population has a larger voice in the county government.

What does the future hold for the city? There is no doubt it will grow, as it has in the past. Current population trends show California will continue to grow and Stockton is a part of that growth pattern. The city has always been flexible, yielding to the tide of events and answering the needs around it. There is no reason to believe this will change.

The words of early settler Charles Grunsky, written in a letter home to Germany on January 19, 1851 proved him to be a prophet:

I may be wrong, but I confess that I have great faith in the future of this beautiful country. I believe that in time it will

As the west end of Stockton progressed through redevelopment and old buildings were knocked down by the wrecker's ball, new buildings were erected in their stead. At the head of the channel the multi-roofed Hotel Stockton continues to dominate the skyline unique to Stockton. Courtesy, City Council Chambers

be the foremost state in the Union. With the resources of this state, tremendous progress can be made. There will soon be talk of a railroad from New York to San Francisco, Sacramento or Stockton. A railroad thousands of miles of which will pass through a vast extent of uninhabited wilderness and will cross the Sierra Nevada.

Here was a man of vision who had faith in the city of Stockton, for he selected it as his home. Others followed and made the city what it is today.

The unique combination of land and water in the Stockton area has attracted man from the beginnings of the region's history. Today Stockton is a cosmopolitan city which accepts new people, never promising a paradise but offering a refuge, where each must earn his place. It is a vital, thriving place where the land nurtures abundance as each day the sun rises over the majestic Sierra Nevada mountain range, reaches its zenith over the city, and sets behind the Diablo range into the sunset sea. It is a place for people—a very special place indeed.

VIII.

PARTNERS IN PROGRESS

By Mel Bennett

During the California Gold Rush days Stockton Channel, stemming some two and one-half miles from the San Joaquin River to mid-Stockton, was the head of navigation for paddle-wheel and side-wheel steamboats and sailing vessels carrying fortune hunters from San Francisco bound for the Mother Lode and High Sierra goldfields. Those gold seekers accounted for Stockton's commercial beginnings by their purchases of picks and shovels, boots and woolens, buggies, wagons and horses, and food—to say nothing of their patronization of local saloons.

Many luckless prospectors returned to chop down thousands of oak trees surrounding Stockton to reap the golden harvests of farming, thus starting the city on its way to becoming the center of one of the ten richest agricultural counties in the nation: San Joaquin County produced nearly $770 million in crops in 1982.

The area's soil yields scores of crops, led by milk, grapes, tomatoes, nuts, and livestock. Early-day flour mills have been replaced by feed mills, corn products, walnut-and meat-processing plants, and canneries and frozen-food plants.

Agriculture led to industry, the first factories manufacturing farm machinery and implements as the pioneers dug for crops rather than gold. Stockton now has 300 industries, producing pleasure cruisers and yachts, illuminated glass, cement pipe, steel-fabricated and wood products, and modules for Alaskan oil fields, to list a few.

Today Stockton is the head of navigation for seagoing cargo ships that dock at the Port of Stockton, the city's first and foremost inland seaport. Created by converting the San Joaquin River into a 30-foot ship channel, it currently is being deepened to 35 feet. Stressing bulk cargo, the port loads and unloads cargoes for ships that sail the seven seas and is served landwise by three transcontinental railroads and 200 trucking lines.

Financial transactions are conducted by several hundred banks, savings and loan agencies, credit unions, and lending agencies that offer all manner of loans, from personal to homeowner, from crop to business, and ranging from $100 to $500,000.

The fine local educational system is enhanced by San Joaquin Delta, a community college, and University of the Pacific, the second-oldest institution of higher learning in California. Stockton boasts theater, ballet, symphony, an art league, and a museum and art gallery for the culturally minded. Sports fans can witness events in all major fields and there are facilities available for tennis, golf, swimming, softball, and bowling, as well as numerous parks for picnicking.

The organizations you will meet on the following pages have chosen to support this important civic event. They are representative of the businesses that have helped to make "Stockton, Someplace Special," with the talent, skills, and determination that are the lifeblood of a thriving community.

Stockton's growth escalated more in the 15 years between 1960 and 1975 than it had in the previous 100 years. This aerial view of downtown Stockton occurred prior to the West End Redevelopment program the city underwent in the mid-1960s and 1970s. Clearly in view is Washington Square, once the location of the Agricultural Pavilion, and to its left is Chinatown. The Civic Auditorium, Hotel Stockton, the back of the courthouse, and Cunningham's Castle (County Jail) are also in view. Courtesy, Stockton Chamber of Commerce

THE GREATER STOCKTON CHAMBER OF COMMERCE

In 1901 three public-spirited Stockton citizens—attorney Oscar Parkinson, superintendent of schools James Barr, and county treasurer W.C. Neumiller—took the initial steps to organize a Stockton Chamber of Commerce, now prefixed with "Greater."

They were determined to create an agency to promote the growth, prosperity, and development of the city of Stockton. Their immediate goal was 300 members, and they named a committee that garnered 600 members at the organization's first meeting on February 27, 1901.

The noble 600 elected banker Fred West as president and hired a permanent secretary for $150 a month and a stenographer for $25 a month. A typewriter was rented for $6 a month and the office rental was $10 a month.

The embryonic group's first project was the endorsement of a $150,000 bond issue for the erection of old Stockton High School, now razed because of earthquake faults. Other Chamber activities over the years include selling Liberty Bonds during World War I; underwriting campaign expenses for the late 1920s bond issue that resulted in a San Joaquin River deep-water channel and the Port of Stockton, California's first inland seaport; urging the establishment of a modern airport, now Stockton Metropolitan Airport; promoting the formation of a mosquito-control district; supporting bond issues to form a Stockton-East San Joaquin Water District; sponsoring both Stockton Ag Expo, a major western farm equipment show, and The Stockton Boat Show; establishing a program to seek out and help emerging leaders develop their potential; and forming Junior

During the 1930s The Greater Stockton Chamber of Commerce sponsored cruises down the San Joaquin River deep-water channel aboard the J.D. Peters, *the last of the paddlewheelers that once plied the river.*

Achievement, a "learn-by-doing" program for students who start their own "companies" under the sponsorship of local firms.

The Chamber also solicits Hollywood movie studios to film in or near Stockton. Some $9 million has been spent filming 40 movies locally, including *Coast to Coast, Cool Hand Luke, The Big Country,* and the steamboat race for Will Rogers' *Steamboat 'Round the Bend.*

Chamber publications are *Port-O-Call,* a tabloid business newspaper, and a membership directory and business guide. The organization's latest project is the sponsorship of this illustrated history of Stockton.

The Greater Stockton Chamber of Commerce has burgeoned, until today there are 1,700 members headed by a 26-person board of directors of volunteer Chamber members, plus a professional staff. Assisting the professional staff are committees on economic development, government affairs, community affairs, trade expositions, membership relations, and Chamber affairs.

GEIGER MANUFACTURING COMPANY

Three generations ago Geiger Manufacturing started serving local industries. Today its work can be found throughout the United States. For the past 15 years this firm, which builds machinery to its customers' design as well as its own, has been managed by Carolyn Geiger.

It all began in 1904 when Joseph Geiger, a machinist at the old Sampson Iron Works, started the Geiger Iron Works, a jobbing machine shop, on West Weber Avenue, just off Stockton Channel. Most of the early work involved making machines for the former Holt Manufacturing Company. However, Geiger found time to design and construct an asphalt paving plant that contributed to the development of paved highways in California to replace the old dirt roads.

When the Weber Avenue shop was destroyed by fire in 1913, Geiger moved his operations to the present site at 1110 East Scotts Avenue. A community-minded Geiger served on the commission that was successful in establishing, in 1933, California's first

Joseph Donald Geiger was president of Geiger Manufacturing during World War II, when the firm produced practice bomb casings for the United States Armed Forces.

inland deep-water port on Stockton Channel, not far from Geiger's original shop.

Geiger, who had a way with words as well as tools, one day was accosted by an employee who said, "I think I'm worthy of a raise." The master machinist replied: "Some days you're worth it; some days you're not. Today you're not." Company records reveal that in 1910 the total monthly pay of

the firm's seven employees amounted to $444.60, about $100 less than the average weekly pay of each of today's 22 employees.

By the time of Geiger's death in 1930 the business had been incorporated. His widow assumed the presidency, serving until 1936, when she was succeeded by their son, Joseph Donald Geiger, who had reached industrial management age.

During World War II the firm manufactured practice bomb casings and submarine doors and young Geiger was instrumental in forming the Stockton Manufacturers' Association for producing machinery and other heavy equipment for the Mare Island Navy Yard.

During the period of his management the company grew and greatly expanded its machining capabilities to become the largest jobbing shop in the valley. When Joseph Donald Geiger died in 1969 ownership and management passed to his widow, Carolyn.

Over the years Geiger has produced tomato and celery transplanters, silk-screen printing presses, paper box folders, machine bottle washers and fillers, and can making and mining equipment. Geiger Manufacturing currently is developing a selective asparagus harvester. Inquiries about this self-propelled harvester that cuts three rows of "grass" at one time have been received from growers in California, Washington, Alabama, Michigan, England, and Australia. Geiger Manufacturing continues to explore new fields where the company can use the talents of its skilled machinists to develop new products.

Geiger Manufacturing—a part of Stockton's past and a participant in its future.

The Geiger crew in the mid-1910s, with founder Joseph Geiger (far right, wearing derby).

ALPINE PACKING COMPANY

Since 1936 Stockton's Alpine Packing Company has produced hams and bacon, sausages, and hot dogs to please the palates of thousands—perhaps millions—of people in Central California.

But there seems to be a question as to whether founder Joseph Kaeslin—"just call me Joe"—named his meat-processing plant for the famed Alps of his native Switzerland. Even today, the now-retired Kaeslin answers queries with: "I don't remember," and, after a pause, adds, "I just thought it would be a good name."

Born in 1909 in a small town on the shores of Switzerland's Lake Lucerne, Kaeslin, as a boy, did farm chores and milked cows. Eventually, despite an ambition to become an auto mechanic, Kaeslin learned the art of sausage making in the city of Lucerne, where he lived with the family who operated the sausage kitchen to which he was apprenticed.

However, in 1930, at the age of 21,

Joe Kaeslin (right), founder of the Alpine Packing Company, poses with the trophy he won in 1975 for outstanding achievement in the meat industry. At left is Norman Maffit, vice-president of the Western Meat Packers' Association.

he decided to seek his fortune and future in the United States and after a grueling 7,000-mile journey by ship and train he arrived at the Modesto, California, home of his sponsor, Werner Kaiser, a family friend who had immigrated to America several years before.

Despite the fact that the United States was in the throes of the Great Depression, the young man did not have any trouble finding

employment. Successively he did farm work near Banta, made sausage in San Francisco, baled hay in Dos Palos, and made sausage for the old El Dorado Meat Market in Stockton.

Kaeslin not only became El Dorado Meat's only sausage maker but butchered and cured meat and handled every facet of the trade—all of which held him in good stead later in establishing one of the Central Valley's outstanding meat-packing and -processing plants, Alpine Packing Company. For a time in 1933 Joe Kaeslin, who was fast learning the English language, was Stockton's only sausage maker remaining when the Wagner Meat Company, which employed two, closed down.

During his Stockton days Kaeslin became a partner in two sausage-making businesses, the first of which, the Port Stockton Sausage Company, became a minor disaster. He left the partnership when he discovered that his two partners had incorporated the business in a move to freeze him out.

But Kaeslin hit the jackpot in his second partnership venture. In 1936, after a short sausage-making spell in Sacramento, Kaeslin returned to Stockton and with two partners purchased the failing Elk Meat Company. They formed the Delta Sausage Company at 107 North American Street in facilities formerly occupied by the Port Stockton Sausage Company.

But Kaeslin's partners—one seemed to love gambling and the other loved the ladies—turned out to be more hindrance than help. So, in September 1937, Kaeslin bought them out and established himself as the sole owner of a sausage factory— or better, kitchen—which he revised and rechristened the Alpine Packing Company.

This aerial view shows the extensive plant and yards of the Alpine Packing Company on Lower Sacramento Road just north of Stockton.

Displaying a prize-winning steer at the San Joaquin County Fair's 4-H Club and Future Farmers of America auction are Joe Kaeslin (center), an Alpine employee, and the steer's young owner (right).

On New Year's Eve of 1936 he drove through the snow to Reno, where he was married to Laura Prima, a pretty young southern woman from New Orleans whom he had wined and dined (on a bet) and dated while she was the bookkeeper during his brief employment at the Port Stockton Sausage Company.

At first Alpine was a small

Although retired since 1978, founder Joe Kaeslin visits the firm's plant almost daily "just to keep in touch."

operation in the sausage kitchen on American Street, with Kaeslin marketing the products from a panel truck and making collections on his way home. Alpine expanded when Kaeslin was joined by Cassius Rollin "Bob" Knoles, brother of Dr. Tully C. Knoles, former president of College of the Pacific, now a university. Bob Knoles had sold his interest in the Port Stockton Sausage Company to Kaeslin when illness caused him to go to Arizona.

Alpine broke ground for a modern, spacious plant at Miner Avenue and Aurora Street on December 8, 1941, the day after the bombing of Pearl Harbor. Business continued to expand at the Miner-Aurora plant but there was a need for slaughtering facilities. So, in November 1949, Kaeslin, at a bankruptcy sale, purchased the slaughterhouse and 129-acre tract of the Salcedo Meat Company on Lower Sacramento Road. Sausage making continued at the Miner-Aurora plant for five years.

Today the 9900 Lower Sacramento site houses several buildings covering 50,000 square feet, with common

walls, for the manifold meat-processing operations such as slaughtering, sausage making, and boning. Also on the tract is a large corral for livestock received at the plant in Alpine Packing trucks.

Currently, Alpine slaughters some 60,000 head of cattle annually for carcass sales to California retail butchers and purveyors who convert the beef into steaks and other cuts in Central California, the Bay Area, and Los Angeles. Alpine processes 15,000 to 16,000 hogs each year, which the packing company converts into hams, sausages, and fresh pork cuts, including wieners and bologna. Alpine produces approximately four million pounds of sausage and luncheon meats and one million pounds of ham and bacon each year.

All Alpine products are United States Department of Agriculture-inspected. There is little waste at the company—the hides of slaughtered animals are sold to tanneries, and inedible items are sold to a tallow-rendering company.

Today the firm sells $35 million in beef and pork products annually, compared to $50,000 in sales the first year; has 75 employees with a $1.5 million payroll, compared to that three-man operation in 1936; hauls livestock from California, Oregon, and Nevada; and delivers processed meat in 20 trucks and trailers, compared to a lone panel truck in the early days.

Alpine Packing Company is a family operation, with the retired Joe Kaeslin continuing as president and his wife Laura serving as treasurer. A son, Joseph L. Kaeslin, is first vice-president; another son, Dennis L. Kaeslin, is second vice-president; and a daughter, Alice L. Kaeslin, is secretary.

HICKINBOTHAM BROS. LTD.

Today's traffic jams are nothing new to Stockton.

Back in the 1890s slow-moving horse-drawn streetcars and heavy freight drays blocked Main Street so often that the pioneer Hickinbotham Bros. was forced to move to a less-traveled street.

In 1852 the brothers Hickinbotham, John Tunnicliff and Edwin, established a wagon- and carriage-building shop on Main Street between California and Sutter streets, once the hub of Stockton's business district. In 1860 the firm changed from carriage making to selling wagon- and carriage-making materials.

In 1894, after 42 years on Main Street, the shop was moved to the 500 block of East Market Street where it remained until 1931. At that time operations were established in a building of the former Holt Manufacturing Company, creator of the Caterpillar tractor tread.

The early years' stress was on lumber products but after World War I the company diverted to steel production and today sells steel—cut to size, punched with holes, or bent to meet the customers' needs. Hickinbotham Bros. also distributes industrial and welding supplies and offers production processing such as shearing, saw cutting, flame cutting, rolling, and forming.

There were sales to the gold mines during the brief gold-mining revival in the 1930s but sales have dropped with the price of gold. During World War II Hickinbotham Bros. entered

Don Hickinbotham—president and chief operations officer of Hickinbotham Bros. Ltd. of Stockton.

Ralph Hickinbotham, Jr.—chairman of the board and chief executive officer of the firm.

into a joint venture with Guntert & Zimmerman, known as Hickinbotham Bros. Construction Div., for construction of landing craft, floating cranes, steel tugs, and supply vessels for the war effort.

Most of the firm's current sales are to agricultural-related industries, food processing, the construction and logging industries, and government agencies and the military. The sales area extends from the San Francisco Bay area into Western Nevada and from the Oregon border to Bakersfield.

A period of intense corporate growth occurred in 1977, with the acquisition of the assets and inventory of the Federal Steel and Supply Company of Fresno, giving Hickin-

Hickinbotham Bros., which then specialized in material for wagon and carriage making, occupied this building in the 500 block of East Market Street, Stockton, for more than 40 years. Photo from the L. Covello Photo Collection.

botham Bros. branches in Sacramento, Santa Rosa, and Fresno.

The genealogy of this pioneering family business starts in 1852 with the founding brothers, John Tunnicliff and Edwin Hickinbotham. Following John's death in 1893—brother Edwin had died in 1891—his three sons, George West, John Edwin, and James Henry Hickinbotham, assumed the operation. When James died in 1930 he was succeeded by his three sons, Cyrus, Leland, and Ralph, who converted the business into a corporation, Hickinbotham Bros. Ltd. The last of the trio, Ralph, died in 1951.

Today two fourth-generation grandsons of co-founder John direct the business—Ralph Hickinbotham, Jr., chairman of the board and chief executive officer, and Don Hickinbotham, son of Cyrus, president and chief operations officer. The Hickinbotham dynasty should continue, as Ralph and Don Hickinbotham between them have four sons (one, Ralph III, manages the Santa Rosa branch), two daughters, two sisters, and two nephews.

Like England, there always will be a Hickinbotham.

FREEMAN, RISHWAIN & HALL

Maxwell M. Freeman and Robert J. Rishwain, senior partners in the Stockton law firm of Freeman, Rishwain & Hall, founded the concern in 1964, while Jerry D. Hall, senior partner, joined in 1971. The firm currently has a staff of 27, including 12 attorneys, and there are 5 partners.

Freeman completed his undergraduate work at Stanford University and was graduated from Stanford's School of Law. Rishwain completed his undergraduate work at Stanford University and was graduated from the University of Santa Clara Law School. Hall completed his undergraduate work at the University of California and was graduated from its School of Law.

The first office of the then-Freeman & Rishwain law firm was in Hunter Square Plaza in downtown Stockton, and in 1981 the firm expanded into its present office complex at 1818 Grand Canal Boulevard in the fast-growing northwest Stockton area.

Freeman, Rishwain & Hall is engaged in a general practice, and concentrates on business and personal litigation, real estate law, corporate matters, estate planning, eminent domain, and limited criminal cases.

Over the years, the firm has been active in real estate investments and developments with clients and investors. Developments and investments include residential properties, retirement homes, convalescent hospitals, commercial properties, and warehousing in the western region of the United States.

Freeman, Rishwain & Hall believes in an aggressive and progressive posture for the best interest and financial betterment of its clients.

The firm's members maintain active memberships in the Greater Stockton Chamber of Commerce, the Better Business Bureau, the Credit Bureau of Stockton, and numerous other civic and charitable organizations.

Maxwell M. Freeman

Robert J. Rishwain

Jerry D. Hall

POLLARDVILLE

Once a tiny restaurant, Pollardville, just north of Stockton on Highway 99, now is a three-in-one operation—a chicken-specialty restaurant, a theater/restaurant, and an early western village.

After operating a take-out restaurant in the Castro Valley, Ray and Ruth Pollard in 1947 opened a counter-and-three-table chicken kitchen at Ashley Lane not far from the present location. Pollards' grew to a 100-diner-capacity restaurant specializing in a secret chicken batter created by Mrs. Pollard and prepared on equipment developed by her husband.

In 1957 they erected today's Chicken Kitchen, with a 250-diner capacity, and moved the original building to the rear, to serve as a banquet room. The industrious couple then moved a building from the old Thornton Cannery next to the Chicken Kitchen and converted it into a museum to house the antiques they had collected—old music boxes, player pianos, buggies, and even a fire engine.

In 1958, when filming of *The Big Country* in the nearby Farmington area was completed, the Pollards purchased the sets—a hotel, saloon, general store, and barber shop—which became the beginnings of Ghost Town, a replica of an early western town. The addition of walls, roofs, and floors converted the set fronts into usable facilities.

Actual historic buildings acquired for Ghost Town include a 20- by 20-foot brick structure that once was the Jamestown jail, a saloon interior from St. Helena, and a tiny six- by eight-foot post office that once served the Sierra village of Mountain Ranch. A former Lodi freight station now serves a half-mile narrow-gauge railroad with

Pollardville's Ghost Town brings back memories of early towns of the Old West, featuring authentic and movie set buildings.

The late Ray Pollard founded Stockton's Pollardville in 1957.

its miniature locomotive and two passenger cars and track salvaged from an abandoned Grass Valley area mine.

Some of the antiques were moved to Ghost Town and other areas of Pollardville in 1965, when the museum was converted into a theater, the Pollardville Palace, now the Palace Showboat Dinner Theatre. The theater, whose seating capacity was increased from 180 to 280, features old-time melodramas and vaudeville,

with dinner served at 7 p.m. and an 8:30 curtain time. Two shows are presented yearly with each show running approximately six months.

Typical "melodramas," some of them written locally and others from play services, have been *The Drunkard, Shoot Out at Hole-in-the-Wall,* and *The Rat Catcher's Daughter.* Naturally, the audience is invited to boo the villain, cheer the hero, and shed tears for the damsel in distress. Local thespians who have participated in Show Boat productions include Ray Rustigian, Phil and Monica DeAngelo, Lloyd and Janet Wessling, and choreographer Lavergne Balk.

Ray Pollard, who died in 1976, was preceded in death by his wife, Ruth, in 1967. Succeeding in active management of Pollardville are sons Neil and Gary, whose partners in the family-owned corporation are a sister, Marie Jobe of Lodi, and a brother, Dudley Pollard, of Del Mar. Neil's wife Doris manages the dinner theater, while son Gregory assists in theatrical productions and a daughter, Linda, is a restaurant hostess.

ST. JOSEPH'S HOSPITAL

The story of St. Joseph's Hospital of Stockton is one of response to community need. In 1898 Father William O'Connor established a home for old men—a place where care and comfort would be provided for those in need of a home. From the beginning local physicians prevailed upon Father O'Connor to include a hospital in his project. With considerable community support, St. Joseph's Home and Hospital opened on December 21, 1899, on a five-acre tract in the 1800 block of North California Street—the gift of Julia Weber, daughter of the founder of Stockton, Captain Charles M. Weber.

The foresight of the hospital's founder was apparent at once. While the complex included the hospital, buildings for the men's home, as well as kitchen and dining facilities, it also contained a residence for the Dominican Sisters who were to staff the facility. The enthusiasm of community physicians for Father O'Connor's Home and Hospital assured the growing city of Stockton that its first private medical care facility would be successfully implemented.

Father O'Connor administered St. Joseph's until his death in 1911. A bronze statue of this caring and thoughtful priest graces the hospital grounds today, a symbol of the founding spirit that is yet present. In 1912 the Dominican Sisters were given the responsibility for administering the facility. Under their stewardship St. Joseph's Hospital has grown into a distinguished comprehensive health care organization.

Over the years, St. Joseph's has expanded greatly. A two-story building was erected in 1916, with a third floor added in 1926, and a wing in 1954. Multimillion-dollar expansions were accomplished in 1962, 1965, 1970, and 1976. Today St. Joseph's Hospital is a 316-bed acute care facility with a sophisticated emergency department open 24 hours a day to treat major illness or trauma. This service was complemented in 1983 with the opening of an immediate care center on March Lane, in North Stockton.

St. Joseph's Hospital, which is accredited by the Joint Commission on Accreditation of Hospitals, installed the first cardiac defibrillator in the San Joaquin area in 1957 and in 1967 recorded another first with the implementation of a cardiac care unit. Also for heart patients, the hospital offers cardiac surgery and cardiac rehabilitation programs. A regional medical center, the hospital is well known for its pulmonary and trauma care, its medical, surgical, maternity, pediatric, and crisis intervention units. As well, St. Joseph's has an accredited cancer program, providing radiation therapy, oncology, and social services. Additional services also include home health care, short stay surgery, a learning center, and physical and occupational therapy.

The hospital operated a nurses' training school from 1902 to 1938, and in the 1950s a vocational nursing

An aerial view of St. Joseph's Hospital. The facility grew from a home for the elderly to an ultra-modern hospital on the original site.

program was replaced by a registered nursing program in conjunction with San Joaquin Delta College. Services of the auxiliary, organized in 1957, include a gift shop, escort and information services, delivery of mail, flower service, newspapers to patients, and assistance with special events.

Since 1973 the board of trustees has been the governing body of the hospital. Under the direction of Sister Mary Gabriel, president, and Edward G. Schroeder, executive vice-president, St. Joseph's has become a complex organization moving stride for stride with the rapidly advancing medical field. This has necessitated the studied expansion of facilities and services, the development of a staff of nearly 1,500 employees, and the services of a medical staff of 300 physicians.

Original St. Joseph's Home and Hospital buildings, vintage 1905.

NEUMILLER & BEARDSLEE

If the newspaper axiom "names make news" holds true, the law firm of Neumiller & Beardslee is exceedingly newsworthy: In more than 80 years of operation it has had as many name changes as California's weather. In spite of its many name changes the firm has been consistent since 1903 in providing legal services for many area businesses and farmers.

While working at the Farmers Union Milling Co. (later the Sperry Flour Co.), Charles L. Neumiller studied law at night and later graduated from Hastings College of Law in 1901. After a year as assistant to District Attorney Arthur Ashley, Neumiller in 1903 founded with Ashley the law firm of Ashley & Neumiller. Originally located in Hunter Square, the venture later moved to the Hale Building at Sutter and Main streets.

After the partnership was dissolved in 1910, Neumiller practiced with associates until 1915 when he and George Ditz formed Neumiller & Ditz. The office was then moved to the Commercial Savings & Loan Building, later the Bank of America Building.

In 1903 Charles L. Neumiller, two years out of Hastings College of Law, formed the law firm of Ashley & Neumiller with partner Arthur Ashley.

Neumiller, once chairman of the California State Republican Committee, died at San Quentin in 1933 while functioning as a member of the California Prison Board. Ditz was a trustee of Stanford University.

Firm associates from 1913 to 1924 included Edward E. Breitenbucher, later a police judge; and David Lyman, who left to start an accounting firm. Irving Neumiller, nephew of Charles Neumiller, became a partner in 1925; Robert Beardslee in 1941; and when Dudley Sheppard affiliated in 1945, the firm became Neumiller, Ditz, Beardslee & Sheppard. After World War II the name grew still

longer as additional partners joined the firm. The name was trimmed to Neumiller & Beardslee in 1972 and offices were moved to 6 South El Dorado Street in 1976, and to the Waterfront Office Towers, 509 West Weber Avenue, in 1983.

The firm is proud of its past and present involvement with the growth and development of Stockton and the San Joaquin Valley. Neumiller & Beardslee assisted with legal efforts which brought the Western Pacific Railroad to Stockton in 1910 and was also involved in the formation of Holt Manufacturing Co., a forerunner of the Caterpillar Tractor Co. Neumiller & Beardslee served as counsel for State Savings & Loan Association, now American Savings, during its formative period and continues to be proud to be associated with what is now one of America's largest financial institutions.

During the period of Stockton's most rapid growth, the firm served as counsel for various developers such as the Grupe Company and Barnett-Range. As counsel for the Stanislaus River Flood Control Association, Neumiller & Beardslee was deeply involved in the successful 20-year fight to secure the construction and filling of New Melones Dam. As attorney for SDI Community Developers, Neumiller & Beardslee assisted extensively with the Waterfront Redevelopment Project, where the firm's office is now located.

Neumiller & Beardslee was incorporated in 1981. The current principals are Thomas J. Shephard, Sr., Duncan R. McPherson, Rudy V. Bilawski, Robert C. Morrison, James R. Dyke, James A. Askew, and John W. Stovall. Robert L. Beardslee, now counsel, remains active after more than 50 years with the firm.

Associate Judge Edward I. Jones, left, and attorney Charles L. Neumiller, far right, pose with their office staff around 1910.

SDI COMMUNITY DEVELOPERS

Ever since its founding in 1973 by Eckhard Schmitz, who came to the United States as a student from his native Germany in 1968, the then-Schmitz Development, Inc., has been dedicated to the construction of what might be aptly called mini-communities.

The founder, who brought graduate-level academic credentials from the University of Geneva, completed his graduate studies at Stockton's University of the Pacific. While attending University of the Pacific, Schmitz became acquainted with a prominent Stockton real estate developer and on completion of his advanced studies spent several years in the developer's employ serving as coordinator of building, property manager, controller, and finally vice-president of finance and development.

This combined academic and practical operational experience— plus a background of formal management training in a Swiss watch-manufacturing company—led to the creation of what is now known as SDI Community Developers with Schmitz as president. SDI Community Developers adheres to the following economic credo: "The purpose of the business is to develop, own, and operate high-quality communities at a profit."

SDI-planned communities, which have won national and local recognition, conform to certain strict criteria such as uniqueness in character, high quality, and diversified land use coordinated with the environment. Such planned communities, combining a number of land uses into a single concept, can include single-family homes, condominiums, garden and retirement apartments, professional offices, shopping or specialty centers, recreational areas, and open spaces.

Among SDI's total community developments are Venetian Gardens, a $60-million, 156-acre development which includes an attractive arched entrance to St. Mark's Plaza and its markets, restaurant, and a variety of shops and offices, backed by apartments; Venetian Bridges, a $70-million, 139-acre project which includes the glass-covered Bridges Specialty Center and the Stockton Hilton, a deluxe 200-room hotel (300 rooms in 1984) with convention facilities and shops; and The Waterfront, a $100-million, 70-acre community development adjoining downtown Stockton which has brought some 2,000 local residents back to the shores of historic Stockton Channel, where it all began in 1850. Dominating The Waterfront

A landmark grain and flour warehouse was restored to create The Warehouse, a specialty center in The Waterfront community on Stockton Channel.

development of retirement and garden apartments, office buildings, commercial enterprises, and a modern yacht harbor is a huge specialty center, The Warehouse. The building was erected in 1891 by the old Sperry Flour Company for the storage of grain and flour, the latter for shipment to the San Francisco Bay area on the paddlewheel steamers of yesterday. The old Nippon Hospital and the Granary Tower are among the landmark buildings restored for current use.

SDI, which has more than 100 employees, does more than $35 million in construction annually, most of it in Stockton, and its scores of projects have created one thousand permanent and several thousand temporary construction jobs.

SDI's Grand Canal Apartments in the Venetian Bridges community consist of 262 units.

CALIFORNIA CEDAR PRODUCTS COMPANY

Although Stockton's California Cedar Products Company frequently is referred to as "the pencil factory," about the only place pencils are available there is in the business office. Actually, California Cedar Products does not make pencils but does produce cedar slats from which wood-cased pencils are manufactured.

More than 70 percent of the world's pencil manufacturers rely on California incense-cedar (*Libocedrus decurrens*) from the forests of the California Sierra Nevada and the Oregon Cascade mountain ranges. Incense cedar is considered the most acceptable wood for pencils because it is soft — it whittles easily — and has straight grain and uniform texture. Then, too, it is in fairly plentiful supply, constituting about six percent of the Sierra Nevada and Cascade forests, and the trees are prolific and a renewable resource.

Transformation of a tall tree into a tiny pencil is a lengthy, involved, and interesting process that starts in Sierra Nevada and Cascade lumber mills at Mt. Shasta and Pioneer, California, and Roseburg, Oregon, where the cedar logs are cut into three-inch by three-inch squares running eight to 16 feet long, dried, and then shipped to California Cedar for processing into pencil slats.

The company's processing

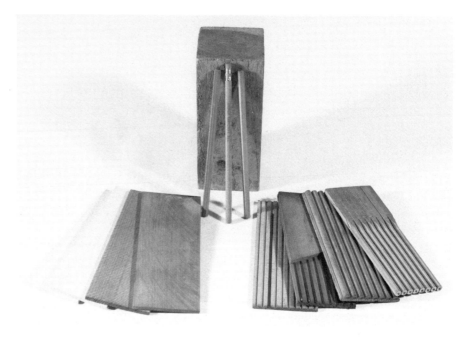

operations begin with the cutting of the "squares" into blocks 7 1/4 inches long, the length of the standard pencil. These blocks then are sawed into slats 2 3/4 inches wide and 3/16th of an inch thick, after which they are impregnated with wax and dyed a reddish color. Waste sawdust is burned in boilers to produce steam and heat to dry the slats. Then follows a final quality-control inspection with electronic machines, and packaging in cardboard boxes — 760 slats to a

This is the saw department of the firm's research laboratory, where many time- and labor-saving machines and processes are developed.

"Evolution of a pencil"—from slats cut from a cedar block by California Cedar to grooving, sandwiching, and the finished product from the pencil factory.

box — enough to make 3,420 pencils.

California Cedar also produces Duraflame™ synthetic fireplace logs that generally outburn wood logs — a minimum of three hours' burning time — primarily from the waste of the pencil-slatting process. Naturally, nationwide sales of Duraflame™ vary with the weather — the colder the better — but company records show that 1978 was a banner year with the sale of 36 million logs, all bearing "Stockton, California," as the source.

The organization's research department over the years has produced an extremely thin saw blade that increased the number of slats sawed from a block, from 10 to 12, a saw tipping machine, an automatic high-speed electronic testing machine, and other labor- and time-saving devices and techniques that have attracted visiting pencil manufacturers from all over the world.

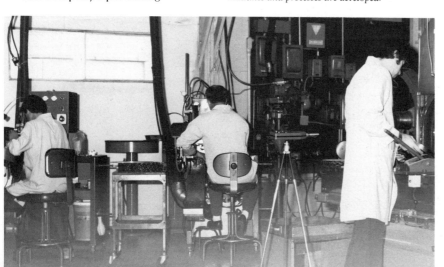

California Cedar, the largest and one of the few remaining pencil slat producers in the United States, was started at its present site in 1919 by W.B. Thurman. He sold out to local interests in 1927 after rebuilding because of a disastrous fire in 1925 that destroyed much of the plant. Since the late 1920s California Cedar has been owned and operated by a family corporation.

The firm, which has 500 employees, has expanded to a 10-acre tract near the Port of Stockton which contains open and covered storage, kilns, waste bins, and facilities housing such departments as milling, treating, sorting, quality control, and the Duraflame™ log plant. The research laboratory is located across town on Waterloo Road.

In the beginning California Cedar processed some 250,000 pencil slats daily—enough for 750,000 pencils. By 1983 daily production had risen to four million slats—enough for 14 million pencils. That adds up to three billion pencils a year.

The slats are then shipped to approximately 16 United States pencil factories and to more than 150 customers throughout the world. All but two of the United States pencil factories are located east of the Mississippi River and slats are shipped to nations in North, Central, and

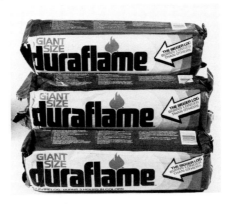

Synthetic fireplace logs are produced from the waste of pencil slat processing at the company's Stockton plant.

South America, Europe, Asia, Africa, and Australia, with the exception of Russia, which uses white pine in its pencils, and China, which utilizes mostly basswood. Brazil uses several of its own local woods.

After the slats arrive at the pencil factories, they are grooved, the "lead" (really a combination of graphite and clay) is laid into the grooves, each leaded slat is covered and glued to another grooved slat to make a sandwich, and the sandwiches are dried. After pressing and drying, the sandwiches are end-trimmed and then

The plant of California Cedar Products Company, producer of pencil slats and synthetic fireplace logs, spreads over five acres near the Port of Stockton.

cut to an appropriate contour to make pencils of round, hexagonal, triangular, or other cross-sections of various diameters.

California Cedar maintains an office in London for European sales and agency offices in Tokyo for its Asian business. The London office is in an alley called King's Court, reputed to have been the home of the infamous Nell Gwynne, intimate friend of King Charles II. Many foreign sales are made by personal visits from the main Stockton office.

Waste is negligible at California Cedar. Most of the waste products fuel the boilers for the kilns, while some shavings and sawdust are converted into wood fiber and sold to paper pulp mills. Perhaps the most energy-efficient by-product is credited to the company's research laboratory, which in 1969 mixed ground wood fiber with petroleum wax and salt to form the principal ingredients of synthetic fireplace logs, manufactured and marketed under the Duraflame™ trade name.

Today there are many varieties of wood-cased pencils—cosmetic, indelible, artist's, colored, carpenter's, printer's, charcoal, and the common variety used to tackle crossword puzzles, figure out income taxes, compile a shopping list, or dash off an informal note.

CONNELL MOTOR TRUCK COMPANY

The Connell Motor Truck Company is to trucks as a doctor is to his patients: It repairs physical damage, treats service malfunctions, and seeks to prolong "life."

The enterprise, now located at 2211 North Highway 99 (Wilson Way), was started in the 1930s by Ed Garvey and James Connell, a pair of ambitious auto mechanics, at 5 East Miner Avenue in downtown Stockton. The original business stressed the sale and servicing of heavy-duty truck equipment culminating, in 1939, with its appointment as the first-ever retail dealer representing Peterbilt Motors Company, which was then manufacturing trucks at what had been the old Fageol plant in Oakland, California.

The year 1946 was a year of change for the company. The Garvey-Connell partnership was dissolved and Connell's operations were moved to the present Highway 99 site. The newly renamed Connell Motor Truck Company, a family corporation with James Connell as president, continued to expand with the formation of a

Connell's main service and parts departments are fully equipped and stocked to service truckers' needs.

This early photo shows a service station adjoining the main service shop of the Connell Motor Truck Company at 2211 North Highway 99.

subsidiary corporation: Lift Truck Service Corporation in 1951. Today Lift Truck Service Corporation, with branches in Stockton, Sacramento, Fresno, and Modesto, deals in the service, sales, parts, and rentals of all types of materials-handling equipment, representing the Yale product line in each of those locations. Since 1955 Connell has owned and operated a complete branch, representing Peterbilt in sales, service, and parts for all types of heavy-truck equipment in a physical facility contiguous to its Fresno lift truck branch.

The Highway 99 tract, expanded to 15 acres from the original five, houses Connell Motor's 37,200-square-foot main service shop, an office building, a service station, a barber shop, and a restaurant, along with ample yard storage and service space. Starting with 20 workers, the Connell Motor

Truck Company currently has 47 employees in Stockton and 19 in Fresno, while Lift Truck Service employs 20 in Stockton, 15 in Sacramento, 14 in Modesto, and 13 in Fresno.

On the death of James Connell in 1960, his widow, Wilma Connell, assumed the presidency of the family corporation. Upon a subsequent recapitalization in 1971, her son by a previous marriage, Gordon T. Egan, former executive vice-president, became president.

Active in public life as well as in trucking affairs, Egan served as president of The Greater Stockton Chamber of Commerce in 1967-1968, is a past president of both the Downtown Stockton 20-30 Club and the North Stockton Rotary Club, and is a former chairman of the board of the Stockton Metropolitan Transit District. Currently he serves on the boards of directors of Hickinbotham Bros. Ltd. and of the Stockton Savings & Loan Association. He also is a past national chairman—two years—of the American Truck Dealers' Division of NADA.

Meanwhile, Egan and his colleagues find time to administer to the mechanical ailments of Central California trucks from Galt to Bakersfield.

CORN PRODUCTS

They say the corn is greener and taller in Nebraska, which could account for the fact that 90 percent of the corn processed in Corn Products' Stockton corn wet-milling plant comes from the State of the Cornhuskers. The remaining 10 percent processed by the only corn wet-milling operation on the Pacific Coast is grown in the corn fields of San Joaquin County, not far from Corn Products' multimillion-dollar plant on Industrial Drive.

Corn Products' principal products are unmodified starch, used in the manufacture of paper and corrugated boxes, and high-fructose corn syrup (HFCS), used as a sweetener by food and beverage processors, canners, confectioners, bakers, and other manufacturers. Among the firm's other products are high-protein corn gluten feed, corn gluten meal, and steepwater, an ingredient for animal feeds.

There is little waste at Corn Products: Corn germ is processed at other locations where the oil is extracted for use in the production of cooking and salad oil. After the oil is removed, the corn germ meal is sold as a cattle feed supplement.

The Stockton plant—a 59,000-square-foot processing building, two warehouses, bins and tanks for storage of both the finished product and the unprocessed corn as it is received at the plant, a steeping and evaporating area, and an office and shop facility—was opened in April 1981 on a 45-acre tract purchased from the Western Pacific Railroad. The WP serves the facility with 75-car trains carrying Nebraska corn—some 3,000 cars unloaded annually.

Operating 24 hours daily on a 340-day production year, the plant manufactures 260 million pounds of HFCS, 190 million pounds of

Operations of the corn wet-milling plant of Corn Products are computer controlled and monitored for quality, capacity, and production.

unmodified starch, 140 million pounds of corn gluten feed, and 30 million pounds of corn gluten meal annually. The plant processes nearly 900 tons of corn daily, which adds up to more than 300,000 tons, or 11 million bushels, annually.

Most of the plant production is shipped by trucks to food and beverage processors and companies within a 100-mile radius of Stockton. Some starch travels as far as Oregon and Washington for paper and corrugating industries. The plant, which is computer controlled and monitored for quality, capacity, and production, has about 50 employees, with local trucking firms delivering

the firm's products.

Corn Products' Stockton plant is one of four corn wet-milling operations of CPC International in the United States. The other three corn wet-milling plants include Winston-Salem, North Carolina; Argo, Illinois; and North Kansas City, Missouri.

CPC International's total sales rank it as one of the 10-largest food processors and one of the top 100 industrial companies headquartered in the United States. CPC affiliates operate in North America, Europe, Latin America, and Asia, with 107 manufacturing plants in 45 countries.

The multimillion-dollar plant of Corn Products' Stockton corn wet-milling facility on Industrial Drive.

VALLEY ELECTRIC COMPANY

The wiring for the electric lamp by which you are reading this history of Stockton might well have been supplied by the Valley Electric Company of Stockton, one of the leading wholesale electric supply houses in Central California.

What later was to become Valley Electric of Stockton and Valley Electric of Modesto had its start in Sacramento in 1921 as the C.H. Carter Company. In the mid-1920s C.H. Carter opened a branch in Stockton which was to continue under his name until 1945 when the firm was split into separate companies—the Valley Electric Company of Stockton and the Valley Electric Company of Sacramento. Earl W. Raffety, who had been with the Stockton branch of the C.H. Carter Company since 1933, became the owner and president of Stockton's Valley Electric, a post he held until his death in 1981.

Meanwhile, in 1978 the Stockton Valley Electric established a separate enterprise in Modesto—a joint venture with H. Lee Dempsey, Jr., and his brother, Larry S. Dempsey.

Lee Dempsey, a graduate of California Polytechnic State University with a bachelor of science degree in engineering and a minor in business management, had been operating out of Sacramento as a field engineer for a national electric firm. Larry Dempsey, a graduate of San Jose State with a bachelor of science degree in industrial management, had been a design engineer in the missiles and space division of the Lockheed Company.

In July 1982, after the death of Mr. Raffety, Valley Electric of Stockton and Valley Electric of Modesto were merged into one corporation, with Lee Dempsey as president and

director of the Stockton operations and Larry Dempsey as vice-president and manager of the Modesto operations.

When Valley Electric, then the C.H. Carter Company, moved to Stockton in the mid-1920s it had three employees in a small building not far from the present plant, at 945 East Lindsay Street. Today the firm utilizes over 60,000 square feet and has more than 65 employees in its two locations.

When the Stockton and Modesto operations were merged in 1982, Valley Electric expanded facilities at both locations to include a computer center for programmable controllers, as well as customer training. Additionally, a new quick-service counter fills orders with a minimum of delay. In 1983 the company added a full line of motors and acquired a motor-rewind shop.

Today Valley Electric distributes over 400 manufacturers' lines, with some 28,000 different items, to industrial plants, commercial projects, factories, and contractors in San Joaquin, Stanislaus, Calaveras, Merced, Amador, and East Contra Costa counties. Major items in the full lines of electrical supplies handled by Valley Electric include motor controls, electrical wiring and cables,

Earl W. Raffety, president from 1933 to 1981, built Valley Electric Company into one of the central valley's largest electrical wholesale distributors.

conduit pipe, wiring devices, electrical distribution equipment, fixtures, lamps, and programmable controllers.

Lee Dempsey attributes the success of the organization to "Earl Raffety's policy of having the inventory on hand to service all the customer's electrical needs." And brother Larry adds, "We promise to keep our commitment to maintaining a substantial inventory of quality lines."

Directing the operation of Stockton's Valley Electric Company are (left) Larry S. Dempsey, vice-president, and H. Lee Dempsey, Jr., president.

HOLT BROS.

Holt Bros. is the exclusive Central California distributorship for Caterpillar crawler tractors.

Harry and Parker Holt, operators of Holt Bros., a construction and farm-equipment dealership at 1521 West Charter Way, not only are the exclusive Central California distributors of Caterpillar tractors—their chief stock-in-trade—they are grandnephews of Benjamin Holt, whose Holt Manufacturing Company developed the Caterpillar track for tractors in 1904.

Holt christened the tractor "Caterpillar" when a photographer, filming a test run, commented that the tractor "crawled like a caterpillar." The crawler track, as it is sometimes called, revolutionized farming, especially in the flaky peat soil of the San Joaquin-Sacramento Delta, by "emancipating the horse." Previously, multi-horse teams had been required to pull the heavyweight combine harvesters of the day.

The fame of the Caterpillar track spread worldwide, and it provided mobility for the world's first military tanks, built by the British for World War I.

The grandfather of the Holt brothers, Charles H. Holt, was vice-president of the Holt Manufacturing Co. while their father, C. Parker Holt, was the treasurer and later executive vice-president of the Caterpillar Tractor Co. The Caterpillar Co. was formed in 1925 by combining the Holt firm with the Best Tractor Co. of San Leandro, now headquartered in Peoria, Illinois.

After completing their education the brothers Holt worked for Caterpillar Tractor Co. dealers—Parker in Modesto and Harry in San Jose and Hollister—in parts departments and

The firm's Stockton headquarters is at 1521 West Charter Way.

as mechanic's helpers, truck drivers, and salesmen. In 1939, a year after their father's death, they started their own dealership, Holt Bros., in Santa Maria.

In 1940 the brothers moved their dealership to Stockton, locating on South Aurora Street just two blocks from the original Holt plant which spread over several city blocks. In 1964 operations were moved to the 100,000-square-foot plant on Charter Way, where 250 workers, including 100 mechanics, were employed. They also opened a branch in Los Baños.

In addition to tractors, Holt Bros. also sells diesel and gas engines for standby and prime power. The company maintains sales, parts, and service departments at the Charter Way plant for the tractors and engines it sells throughout six Central California agriculturally oriented counties.

Engine Power Co., a wholly owned subsidiary of Holt Bros., has a worldwide quality reputation for furnishing dependable installations of prime and standby power for such diverse purposes as pumping oil across 750 miles of Saudi Arabia desert, powering satellite communication stations throughout Algeria and Indonesia, and supplying hospitals and commercial installations nationwide with emergency power.

ON LOCK SAM'S

Bang! Bang! Bang!

Back in the 1920s and 1930s, Stockton's last era as "a wide open town," these almost-continuous and cacophonous sounds were heard by people dining at On Lock Sam's in the heart of the city's Chinatown.

The "bangs" were the slamming of the electrically controlled doors of the gambling joints—there were at least half a dozen on the On Lock Sam's block—when a lookout admitted "visitors" after sizing them up through a screened peephole.

Eventually the gambling joints and houses of ill fame were closed by the government during World War II, when several military installations were located in the Stockton area. And Chinatown was razed in 1964 as part of the west end redevelopment project.

Today On Lock Sam's is located in a pagoda-type building at 333 South Sutter Street and is operated by third-generation grandsons.

A balcony fronted the second-floor On Lock Sam's restaurant on East Washington Street in Stockton's old Chinatown when it was opened in 1898.

Wong Sai Chun came to the United States in 1918 from his native China, first locating in Sacramento where he managed an herb store. In 1920 Wong and two partners, a cook and a noodle maker, acquired On Lock Sam's—which had been serving Chinese food since 1898 on the second floor of a three-story hotel at 125 East Washington Street.

Later Wong bought out his two partners and successfully operated the Oriental eatery until his death in the mid-1950s. At that time his son, Jim Suey Wong, took over. Jim Suey died in 1964, shortly before the building was razed and the restaurant moved to Sutter Street.

His eldest son, Robert Wong, succeeded Jim Suey and a second son, Jenkin Wong, joined him in 1972 in a family corporation partnership with their mother, Lillian Wong, as president. Other shareholders include two cousins of the Wong family, Jimmie and Ruth Wong.

Through the years On Lock Sam's has perfected the Cantonese style of Chinese cooking, considered the finest of the five styles—Peking, Shanghai, Szechwan, Fukien, and Cantonese—and characterized by the "quick" or "toss-fry" method which uses little oil and tends to preserve the natural flavor, texture, and color of the meat and vegetables. Today's restaurant seats 400 diners and there are some 50 employees.

Incidentally, the old East Washington Street restaurant had a brief moment of glory when scenes for the movie, *God's Little Acre*, were shot on the second-floor balcony. Luminaries who have dined with the Wongs include John Wayne, Willie Mays, Paul Newman, Danny Kaye, Ann-Margret, Anthony Quinn, and Michael Landon.

When the South Sutter Street operation was opened every effort was made to preserve the character of the old establishment. The original 1898 On Lock Sam's sign, with its bright gold leaf, marks the entrance to the modern home of Chinese cuisine.

On Lock Sam means "contented heart" and that's what—along with a contented stomach—the Wong family ensure their customers have when they leave their house of Chinese cuisine.

When Stockton's old Chinatown was razed in 1964, On Lock Sam's was moved to this attractive pagoda-style building on South Sutter Street near downtown Stockton.

FRANTZ FILTER COMPANY
LOIS YEE COSMETICS, INC.

The success story of Skipper and Lois Yee has several pertinent facets, to wit: the happy and successful marriage of a Chinese-born youth and a charming co-ed of Japanese ancestry at a time when China and Japan were anything but friendly nations; two separate family corporations operating under the same roof and producing such dissimilar products as automotive oil, fuel filters, and cosmetics; and the assimilation of their two American-born sons into the husband-wife business ventures.

It all started when Yee's father brought his nine-year-old son, Kim Yee (the nickname Skipper came later from a family friend) to the United States and left him with relatives in Phoenix, Arizona. Later coming to Stockton, Yee lived and worked at the YMCA as a towel boy and janitor, served as a physical training instructor with the Air Force in World War II at Stockton Field from 1942 to 1946, and after his discharge from the Air Force enrolled at College of the Pacific, now University of the Pacific (UOP).

It was at Pacific in 1949 that Skipper met and married Lois Kanagawa, born in Sanger, California, of Japanese parents and just out of a relocation center.

While attending Pacific, Skipper was an assistant at Dr. George H. Colliver's Chinese Christian Center and also worked as a recreational therapist at Stockton State Hospital. Following his graduation from Pacific, Yee served two years as trainer for the UOP Tiger athletic teams including the championship football eleven that starred All-American quarterback Eddie Lebaron.

From 1953 to 1959 Skipper sold food supplements and then switched to selling Frantz Filters. The filters,

which use tissue paper as the basic ingredient, are utilized to remove impurities from all oils and fuel.

Skipper liked the product and its potential so well that in 1961 he purchased the Frantz worldwide patents and started manufacturing filters in a plant at 1850 South El Dorado Street. Officially it was the SKY Corporation (Skipper's initials), doing business as the Frantz Filter Company.

Parts built to Skipper's specifications are assembled at the SKY plant and marketed throughout the United States and in 11 foreign countries. Skipper estimates that some three million filters have been sold since 1961.

In 1971 Lois Yee organized Lois

Skipper Yee, his wife Lois, and their sons, Victor and David (left to right) are all actively involved in the Yee family enterprises—Frantz Filter Company and Lois Yee Cosmetics, Inc.

Yee Cosmetics, Inc., for the production and distribution of skin care, hair care, and body care lotions and make-up. At first the products were manufactured by cosmetic companies using Lois Yee formulas. However, the Yee company started making its own products in 1976 when the Yees' chemist son, David, joined the business. Cosmetics also are made for other firms.

In 1977 another son, Victor, created an electronics division for manufacturing beauty care equipment—the major achievement being a painless electronic hair-removing device.

Today the Yee operations continue on an all-in-the-family basis.

The Yee family, Victor, Kathy, Lois, Skipper, Sue, and David (left to right), pose here with the Lois Yee cosmetic line and one of the beauty care machines manufactured by the firm's electronics division.

STOCKTON INN

Guests, greeted by a friendly inn-keeper when they register at the Stockton Inn, are fortunately unaware of the trials and tribulations the motor-hotel experienced in its early days.

In 1969, four years after the Stockton Inn was built at a cost of $1.7 million and operated by Berkroy Development, Inc., of Santa Rosa as a motel and convention center, the inn by the side of Waterloo Road (just off Highway 99) was entangled in owner-ship suits involving a former inn-keeper and a church. However, the resulting arbitration favored Berkroy Development, and the inn continued to operate successfully under J.L. Daniels and Berkroy Development.

Incidentally, during that hectic year of 1969, Stockton Inn gained a degree of prestige and glamour—hosting actor Paul Newman and the cast of his *Cool Hand Luke* movie that was filmed in and about Stockton.

The inn was purchased in 1976 by Western Host, Inc., brainchild of Ronald A. Young, founder and former principal shareholder of Vagabond Motor Hotels (which operates more than 40 facilities) and John F. Rothman, vice-president and general manager of an investment

This lovely lagoon in a garden setting greets the tired traveler driving up to the Stockton Inn for a night of rest and relaxation.

banking firm. Western Host now operates motor-hotels in three western states, with recorded sales of more than $25 million and net earnings of $5 million in 1983.

In 1978 Stanley J. Winkowski, who had operated motor-hotels for Vagabond, was named innkeeper of the Stockton Inn. Previously, Winkowski had been an aerospace engineer with Rockwell International of Los Angeles, where his wife (now his right hand in the Stockton Inn operation) also was employed. At the urging of friends in the hotel-motel field, who said the couple had the right personalities for hosting traveling guests, both resigned from Rockwell and enrolled in the

Anthony School of Hotel and Motel Management.

On graduation from Anthony the Winkowskis were hired by Arnold Engineering and Construction Co. to operate a small motel in Anaheim. On the recommendation of a Vagabond field representative, that position led to larger hotel-motels in Hollywood, Fresno, Rosemead, and eventually Western Host's Stockton Inn.

Winkowski has extensively remodeled the motor-hotel, and has given special attention to the garden-like settings of the 11-acre tract. In addition, a spa has been installed in the area of the inn's original spacious swimming pool. The establishment's 145 rooms are larger than in most hotel-motels, and a homey atmo-sphere prevails in its decor—making it a happy haven for travel-weary businessmen, who create 75 percent of its patronage. Other attributes of the Stockton Inn are a spacious lobby, a 135-guest lounge, a dining room that serves 140, a coffee shop that seats 90, and parking space for more than 300 cars.

Living up to its original billing as a convention center, the Stockton Inn has five small meeting rooms and a large ballroom, and offers accommodations for 15 to 450 con-ventioneers and conferees.

The Stockton Inn, a Western Host motor-hotel, is located at 4219 Waterloo Road, Stockton.

FRANRICA MANUFACTURING, INC.

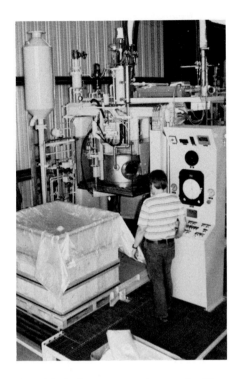

One of the food-processing machines produced by Stockton's FranRica Manufacturing, Inc., is this aseptic bag-filling system designed to fill flexible bags sterilized by gamma radiation.

Stockton's location in the midst of 80 percent of California's fruit and vegetable processing was the prime reason for establishing the FranRica Manufacturing, Inc., a food-processing and -packaging operation, in the then-agriculturally oriented city.

The business was started in 1966 in a 600-square-foot plant on Waterloo Road by Albert Rica—"FranRica" was derived from his father's name—and Lloyd Hay, fellow workers at the Thermovac Company. In 1968 the firm moved to a 25,000-square-foot facility on South 99 Highway, which now houses the main office and assembly operations, while a 30,000-square-foot plant on Hazelton Avenue functions as a fabrication facility.

Also in 1968, FranRica introduced an aseptic drum filler that established the enterprise in the field of food-processing equipment. Developed by Frank and Albert Rica and Lloyd Hay, the drum filler serves as a sterilizer for standard 55-gallon drums for the shipment of tomato paste, puree, sauce, and juices; peach, pear, and apricot purees; and special sauces in a readily usable form. Some 80 of these drum fillers are in use throughout the world today.

The company also produces systems and equipment for aseptic storage of tomato and fruit products, hot fill and cool systems and aseptic systems for flexible packages, specialized heating and cooling systems for particulate products, aseptic flash-cooling systems, and tomato paste evaporators. In addition, FranRica produces an aseptic bag-filling system designed to fill flexible bags sterilized by gamma radiation. Capacities range from one gallon to 300 gallons.

Until 1978 FranRica equipment was used primarily for tomato products processing but now is utilized in an extensive processing range that includes fruits and vegetables, dairy products, and pet foods. The firm maintains a technologies division devoted entirely to research and development of new equipment and market viability studies.

From a small beginning FranRica has developed international status, with use and sales of its machinery and systems in Italy, Peru, Colombia, the Philippines, Egypt, France, Germany, Australia, Argentina, Brazil, Panama, Venezuela, Guatemala, Ecuador, Mexico, Canada, Puerto Rico, Portugal, Spain, Chile, New Zealand, Japan, Taiwan, Korea, Israel, Morocco, Kenya, Russia, Greece, Pakistan, Libya, and South Africa.

FranRica manufactures and sells more than 100 food-processing and

Enhancing the prestige of Stockton's FranRica Manufacturing, Inc., in the production of food-processing and -packaging machinery and systems was this aseptic drum filler built in 1968, two years after the venture was formed.

-packaging machines and systems and annual sales range between $12 and $15 million. The organization has 110 employees, 35 engaged in engineering, sales, and administration, with the remainder serving as assemblers, fabricators, and machinists and performing both field and shop fabrication. A regional office in Chicago serves as a sales center for the Midwest.

Since 1977 FranRica has been a wholly owned subsidiary of Bishopric Incorporated, a Cincinnati holding company, with Albert Rica, son of Frank Rica (who died in 1965), as president and Lloyd Hay as executive vice-president. Steven Rechtsteiner, a former manager of Bishopric's Food Systems Division, serves as vice-president/general manager.

SHEPHERD & GREEN

The history of Shepherd & Green is a tale of two construction firms responsible for many of Stockton's largest and most attractive buildings.

The tale began in 1908 when Jack "Jess" F. Shepherd started a construction business, continuing operations alone until 1918 when he took a partner, Ed Riley. That relationship was dissolved in 1921 and Shepherd continued as the sole operator until his death in 1933. His son, J. Corbin Shepherd, took over the venture at that time and continued under the Shepherd name until the 1937 merger with the firm of Lewis & Green, creating today's Shepherd & Green.

Henry Green died in 1948 but the building firm continues with J. Corbin Shepherd, son of the founder, serving as secretary/treasurer, and his son, John H. Shepherd, who entered the business in 1963, occupying the president's post.

Shepherd & Green erected the seven-story San Joaquin First Federal Building (now known as the Great American Federal Savings and Loan Association Building) in 1975, at a cost of $5 million.

The Green construction phase started in 1910, when Henry Green and Wes Daniels formed a partnership that continued until Daniels' death in 1923. At that time Green became a fellow builder with Tom Lewis until the latter's death in 1937, which led to the merger that created today's Shepherd & Green.

Landmark facilities constructed by Shepherd as a lone builder include the 12-story Medico-Dental Building, now the Sutter Office Center, the McKinley and Fair Oaks schools, and the old Stockton High School Auditorium.

Structures attributed to the Green affiliates prior to the merger include the Southern Pacific Depot, now used for offices only; the 10-story American Savings & Loan Building at Sutter and Main streets, which was the Bank of America Building for many years and originally the Commercial Savings & Loan Bank Building; and the Miner Avenue subway, Stockton's first, under the Southern Pacific and Western Pacific railroad tracks.

Among the Shepherd & Green projects are the Church of the

This imposing 12-story, 120-foot-high Medico-Dental Building, now the Sutter Office Center, was constructed by Jack "Jess" F. Shepherd as an independent builder in the 1920s.

Annunciation and St. Mary's High School; Morris Chapel and the Irving Martin Library at University of the Pacific; the Bank of Stockton complex at Miner Avenue and San Joaquin Street; the San Joaquin First Federal Building at Main and El Dorado streets in a joint venture with Walter A. Hachman, once the site of the pioneer Stockton Theatre (1853-1890); and the Plymouth Square (1972) and Plymouth Place (1982) retirement centers.

For a contrast in architecture and building costs consider the original Medico-Dental Building, 12 stories and 120 feet high, erected in the 1920s, and the 1975 San Joaquin First Federal Building, only seven stories but also 120 feet high. The Medico-Dental Building cost less than $.5 million while the San Joaquin First Federal structure cost $5 million.

Over the years Shepherd & Green and its predecessors have constructed more than $125 million in commercial and industrial facilities, shopping centers, schools, churches, medical centers, and office buildings in Stockton. That proud tradition continues today under the guidance of second- and third-generation Shepherds.

BABKA BEER COMPANY

Although "roll out the barrel" comes from a popular song of yesterday, rolling out the barrels (they call them kegs) is just part of a day's work at Stockton's Babka Beer Company, 1245 West Weber Avenue.

Before coming to Stockton in 1970 to acquire the Pacific Beverage Company and the Coors distributorship, Rink Babka had achieved fame as a discus thrower for the University of Southern California's track and field team. With an all-time best of

This award-winning headquarters of the Babka Beer Company was erected in 1976.

Rink Babka is the owner and operator of Babka Beer Company in Stockton. While a University of Southern California student he was a U.S. discus thrower and won the silver medal in the 1960 Olympic Games in Rome.

217 feet—he was the first man to break the 200-foot barrier—Babka won the Pacific Coast title three times and the national collegiate championship twice.

Following his graduation from USC in 1959, Babka won the AAU national title. His competition had

taken him around the world and in 1960 he took the silver medal in the Rome Olympic Games. Never one to neglect his studies, Babka earned degrees in industrial management and industrial engineering from USC and did graduate work in marketing.

The future beer dealer worked in sales, marketing, and management for computer companies for 11 years despite a youthful ambition to distribute beer. As a youngster he had worked for a beer distributor and dreamed of one day becoming a beer distributor himself—the "American Dream" never afforded his parents who came from Czechoslovakia.

Since realizing his ambition by acquiring the Pacific Beverage Company and Coors distributorship in 1970, Babka has added beer and other malt liquor lines, among them Henry Weinhard, Old English, Grolsch, Warsteiner, Herman Joseph, George Killian, Pabst, and Heileman. He also distributes beers from Holland, Japan, and Germany, as well as mineral waters, soft drinks, and wine drinks. In addition, Babka previously owned and operated the Babka Liquor Company, one of the largest liquor and wine distributors in Northern California, which he sold in 1981. Babka Liquor Company is a member of the California Historical

Society's 100 Year Club.

The firm occupies a 3,500-square-foot Spanish-style office building—an Award of Excellence winner—and a 20,000-square-foot warehouse from which 20 trucks annually deliver one million cases of beer to restaurants, taverns, and liquor, grocery, and specialty stores in cases or half- and quarter-barrels.

Babka also maintains a 5,000-square-foot recycling plant across town, which processes up to 850,000 pounds of aluminum and bottles annually.

In 1980 the Babka Beer Company was named the number one Coors distributor in the medium-size category, and in 1982 was number three overall.

A booster of Stockton's University of the Pacific, Babka served six years as a director of the Pacific Athletic Foundation and is involved in Rotary International, the Boy Scouts, the YMCA, the Children's Home of Stockton, and is a founder of the San Joaquin Youth Soccer League and the International Track Association. Babka was also named to the Southern California Committee for the 1984 Summer Olympics in Los Angeles.

VALIMET, INC.

Valimet, Inc., just south of Stockton on Sperry Drive, has the distinction of producing the smallest industrial item in the Stockton area—in the world, as a matter of fact—metallic spheres not much larger than a particle of dust, which are the constitutional element of metal powders.

The corporation, which has made a valuable contribution to the space program and industry, among other fields, originated as Valley Metallurgical Processing Corporation. In 1974 William Fortman, who had been vice-president in charge of operations for the parent company, came to Stockton as president of Valley. The following year he and Kurt Leopold (a New York financier) purchased the operation, then incorporated with Fortman as president and Leopold as chairman of the board. The firm's name is a rather loose contraction of Valley Metallurgical.

Valimet's spherical aluminum powders originally were developed for use in solid motor fuels for space vehicles—rockets and missiles—in the United States as well as Japan, Sweden, Norway, Germany, England, and France. Expanded endeavors include developing high-strength lightweight alloys for aerospace.

One of the few metallic-powder plants in the world—there are fewer than a half-dozen in the United States—Valimet is the only American, and the world's largest, using the helium-atomizing process for its metallic-powder products. Large quantities of these powders are produced for commercial usage: plasma and flame spraying, diffusion coating, core material for powders, and precipitates for metal recovery from pregnant liquors.

Produced from aluminum, aluminum silicon, aluminum bronze, magnesium, copper, silver, and other metals, Valimet's microspheres provide lower-viscosity mixes, good packing density combined with high chemical reactivity. These properties are advantageous in manufacturing explosives, tracers, and general ordnance.

The Valimet aluminum atomizing towers—the world's largest—can produce, depending on the size of the particles, more than 20 million pounds of powder annually. (It should be noted that pollution-free, inert-gas systems recycle atomizing gases, thus protecting the environment.)

A great percentage of the company's 50 to 75 employees are skilled technicians: metallurgists, chemists, engineers, and laboratory technicians engaged in quality-assurance programs. The staff includes many that were retained when Valley Metallurgical became Valimet in 1975.

The plant, located on an 18-acre tract, consists of 20 buildings with some 45,000 square feet under roof. The powders are shipped in drums by rail, on the firm's own siding; by truck on Highway 99 and Interstate 5; by plane; and by ship through the deep-water Port of Stockton.

Valimet was attracted to Stockton by the mild Central California climate, and its access to transportation by land, sea, and air.

William Fortman continued as president when Stockton's Valley Metallurgical Processing Company became Valimet, Inc., a producer of metallic powders.

Kurt Leopold, a New York financier, is chairman of the board of Valimet, Inc.

FROELIGER MACHINE TOOL COMPANY

Although strictly a local operation, the Froeliger Machine Tool Company, located at 3023 East Myrtle Street in the Fair Oaks industrial area of east Stockton, manufactures tools, dies, and special machines for worldwide marketing—Mexico, Canada, Venezuela, Holland, Israel, Africa, England, and Germany—as well as the United States.

In 1947, after 10 years of apprentice and journeymanship in local plants, Joseph E. Froeliger opened his own shop (about 5,000 square feet) on Gilchrist Avenue, also in the Fair Oaks district, with a fellow worker. Approximately six months later he bought out his partner's interest, and today continues as president of the corporation.

Initially Froeliger designed or helped design special machine tools such as conveyors, palletizers, scale mechanisms, actuating and positioning devices for filling drums with food products, and an automatic squeeze freezer. Over the ensuing years the firm has manufactured tools, dies, and component parts for food processors, canneries, all types of manufacturing plants, steel

fabricators, and, more recently, the fast-growing electronics industry.

From 1950 to 1958 the corporation held $400,000 annually in prime contracts for rebuilding and repairing machine tools for the U.S. Air Force, shipping the tools to McClellan Field near Sacramento. From there they were flown to air bases in the United States and foreign countries. Later government projects have included the manufacture of valves used in space program missiles, and parts for the first atomic-powered submarines built at Mare Island.

Since 1973 operations on Myrtle Street have been executed in a two-facility plant of some 50,000 square feet; a 22,500-square-foot building housing a machine shop and office; and a 27,500-square-foot structure used for fabrication, assembly, and storage.

Major accomplishments include tooling for bin wall retainers, metal walls designed to prevent mountain

After 10 years as an apprentice and then journeyman machinist, Joseph Froeliger started the Froeliger Machine Tool Company.

landslides and to support mountainside roadbeds, tooling for metal revetments at airports, and guard railings for highways.

One of today's foremost products is the Hammel Automatic Carton Stripper, which removes all waste from cartons. The product is named for the late Al Hammel, a co-developer with Froeliger of the stripper. The firm also holds patents on, and manufactures, a drum-closing tool and a companion drum-opening tool.

Appreciative that his apprenticeship enabled him to become a master of his trade, and eventually to own and operate a successful machine-tool company, Froeliger maintains a model four-year apprentice program that earned him a Certificate of Appreciation from the San Joaquin County Joint Apprentice and Training Committee for "outstanding and dedicated service in approved apprentice machinist training."

Also noteworthy is that some of his present employees entered the apprentice program 30 years ago, and are now full-time machinists and tool and die makers.

The Froeliger Machine Tool Company in Stockton's Fair Oaks district has been manufacturing tools, dies, and special machines for worldwide marketing since 1947.

DAY & NITE LOCKS AND SECURITY SYSTEMS

Safety—First, Last, and Always might well be the slogan of two firms operated in Stockton by Charles Skobrak: Day & Nite Locks, and Day & Nite Security Systems. Both organizations are devoted to providing devices, systems, and services designed to protect life, limb, and property.

Skobrak learned the locksmith and other safety trades in his native Hungary, and almost immediately went to work for a lock and key company upon his immigration to the United States and Stockton in 1957. Within five years he originated his own lock and key business at 346 North Stanislaus Street, later moving to 706 North El Dorado Street, and subsequently opening a branch at 6256 Pacific Avenue.

Initially installing locks and making keys, Skobrak soon ventured into burglary alarms and eventually offered burglary- and fire-resistant safes, both

With company vans in the background, the combined crews of Skobrak's Day & Nite Locks and Day & Nite Security Systems pose for this picture.

Charles Skobrak, president of Day & Nite Locks and Day & Nite Security Systems, in 1963, a year after he opened the firm.

old and new, and now alleges to have the largest selection of safes in San Joaquin County. The firm also sells safe-deposit boxes to banks and savings and loan associations, electronic-security devices, access-control systems, and locks and keys for both foreign and domestic automobiles. In addition, 24-hour emergency service is provided for replacing house and car keys.

Beginning as a lone operator in 1962, the founder now has 2 locations, 13 employees, and 5 vans for his lock, key, and safe business.

Due to the tremendous expansion in the residential-, commercial-, and industrial-safety fields, Skobrak in 1973 formed a second company, Day & Nite Security Systems. Located at 708 East Lindsay Street, the operation sells, installs, and services burglary and fire alarms, smoke detectors, access-control systems, electronic-gate controls, hold-up alarms, sprinkler supervision, and elevator emergency-telephone monitoring.

Day & Nite Security Systems is Underwriters Laboratory listed and certified—which means that it is a central station equipped to receive burglar- and fire-alarm signals, both through private telephone lines and digital communicators that identify and record the source and nature of the alarms. The company also installs closed-circuit televisions in buildings such as department stores, banks, and markets, whose cameras cover every section of the business, filming crimes in the act of commission. With approximately 36 employees and 17 trucks, vans, and pickups in operation, the organization has become the largest security firm in the county.

The two Day & Nite companies are separate, incorporated operations with the same officers: Skobrak, president; his wife Donna, secretary/treasurer; and her mother, Lavina Stamos, vice-president. The Skobraks' 19-year-old son, Charles Jr., works full time for the lock and key firm, while 16-year-old Steve is a summer employee.

With a touch of philosophy, Skobrak emphasizes the value of protective devices and systems thusly: "Better a year early than a day late."

ACME TRUCK PARTS AND EQUIPMENT, INC.
ACME TRUCK LIFTS, INC.

Ironically, traffic accidents in Stockton from the 1920s through the late 1950s meant money in the bank for the old Acme Auto Wrecking Company—predecessor of today's Acme Truck Parts and Equipment, Inc., and Acme Lift Trucks, Inc.

The original company bought cars and trucks damaged beyond repair, from which it salvaged vital parts to be sold to motorists at reasonable prices. The enterprise was founded by Sol Davidson, who immigrated to the United States from Russia at the age of six, drove a Model T truck for the family store as a teenager, and was a field ambulance driver during World War I.

Driving the Ford truck so impressed Davidson with motor vehicles that following the armistice

After serving as a field ambulance driver in World War I, Sol Davidson went into the auto-wrecking business in Fresno. He returned to Stockton in 1923 to start the Acme Auto Wrecking Company.

Al Davidson is president of Stockton's Acme Truck Parts and Equipment, Inc., an offspring of the old Acme Auto Wrecking Company.

he and an older brother, Sam, opened an auto- and truck-dismantling and used-car business in Fresno. In 1923 the young entrepreneur returned to Stockton to form the Acme Auto Wrecking Company. An early employee was a 16-year-old brother-in-law, Joe Sweet, who worked after school hours and on weekends, joining on a full-time basis following graduation from high school in 1926; he became Davidson's partner in 1944. Joe Sweet remained active in the business until his death in June 1983.

In those early days the shop was open seven days a week, dismantlers were paid $20 a week, and a good salesman could earn all of $30 in a seven-day work week.

During World War II Acme generated scrap metal for the war effort, and saved parts to keep cars and trucks running despite the

scarcity of replacements.

Davidson's son, Al, entered the business in 1949 as a graduate of the University of California with a bachelor of science degree in mechanical engineering. Young Davidson became a partner when his father died in 1955.

By 1957 the truck and equipment phase had so grown that the auto-dismantling division was sold, and Acme Truck Parts and Equipment, Inc., was born. The following year Sweet's son, C.N. "Bud," who had joined the firm in 1956, helped open a branch in San Jose—Specialty Truck Parts, Inc., which he managed until his boating-accident death in 1974. Both operations are now headed by Al Davidson, chairman of the board; his nephew, Andy Grutman, vice-president; and Roger Stanton, president of Specialty Truck Parts, Inc.

Acme Lift Trucks, Inc., was formed in 1962 to market all-wheel-drive forklifts and other material-handling equipment and hydraulic components. Ken Richardson, who became associated with the parent company at the age of 16, now serves as its president.

Products of all three operations are sold throughout California, as well as nationally and internationally.

The two Stockton plants, across the street from each other on South Wilson Way, have 33,000 square feet of floor space in several buildings and large outdoor storage areas.

Active in community affairs, Joe Sweet was a director of both the Community Center for the Blind and Temple Israel, while Al Davidson has served as a director of the Better Business Bureau, the United Way, Stockton Rotary, and as president of Temple Israel.

DON BLAIR LUMBER CO.

Don W. Blair founded the Don Blair Lumber Co. in 1945 and operated the construction-oriented business until his death in 1980.

To paraphrase a well-known expression, "oil for the lamps of China," it might be said that the Don Blair Lumber Co. of 2001 East Fremont Street provides lumber for the building trades of Central California.

The firm was founded in 1945 by Donald W. Blair, who came to Stockton from Kansas in 1923 to take a job at the old Sunset Lumber Company. Subsequently, he and O.D. Ruse, a fellow Kansan and co-worker at Sunset, formed a partnership and opened the Ruse-Blair Lumber Company on the south side of Charter Way between the SP and WP railroad tracks. They ran their yard there until 1936, when the City of Stockton constructed the subway under those tracks. The lumberyard was moved to the southwest corner of Fremont and Monroe streets and Ruse-Blair operated there until 1945, when the partnership was dissolved. Ruse continued the business under his name, and Don started the Don Blair Lumber Co. at its present location.

In addition to his business activities, Don worked with the carpenter apprenticeship program at the old Stockton High School and served as the first president of the East Stockton Kiwanis Club. As Don's health started to decline in the '70s, his son, Robert, an employee since the opening of the firm, became increasingly involved in the

Robert N. Blair, son of the founder, is president of the Don Blair Lumber Co.

management of the business. Don Blair died in 1980. The company was inherited by Robert and his sister, Mary Anne Henny, who continues as a shareholder. Robert Blair is president and treasurer; his son, William E., is vice-president, secretary, and general manager.

Basically a contractors' lumberyard, Don Blair Lumber Co. sells 90 percent of its products to building contractors for the construction of commercial, industrial, and residential structures in Central California. The firm's market area extends north to Sacramento, south to Porterville, west to Antioch, and east into the Sierra Nevada. However, company records show that Don Blair lumber once was used in a housing project in Anchorage, Alaska.

While lumber now arrives at the firm's yard by rail and truck from sawmills in California, Oregon, Nevada, Washington, Idaho, Montana, and Canada, in the days of the Ruse-Blair operation lumber sometimes came in by barge and schooner, shipped from mills along the north Pacific Coast. As a matter of historical fact, the Ruse-Blair enterprise received shipments of lumber on the *Daisy Gray*—the tiny, wooden lumber-schooner that navigated the newly dredged Stockton deep-water channel down the San Joaquin River in 1933 to open the Port of Stockton.

The Don Blair Lumber Co. operates on a 4.2-acre tract with four sheds and an open-area storage capacity for two million board-feet of lumber. In addition, there is a retail hardware store specializing in builders' hardware, fencing, paints, window units, and other building materials. Blair's knowledgeable staff also assists customers with their building and remodeling problems.

MARTIN FUNERAL HOME

Harry A. Martin, founder of the Martin Funeral Home, operated the mortuary from 1939 until his death in 1978.

The Martin Funeral Home, located at 445 North American Street in Stockton, is still family owned and operated with Jeanie Martin, president and manager; JoAnn Martin Thompson, director (both daughters of Harry A. Martin); and Edna Martin, widow of the founder, also a director.

Harry A. Martin opened the doors of his funeral home on December 3, 1939.

A graduate of the Los Angeles College of Mortuary Science in 1930, Martin served his apprenticeship in an Oakland funeral home; he subsequently worked four years for a Lodi firm before acquiring the present site at 445 North American Street in Stockton in 1939. Realizing that it usually takes a funeral home several years to become economically established, Martin began an ambulance service in 1940—Stockton only had one other at the time— which helped support the mortuary until it was on a paying basis. The service, which was discontinued in the early '50s, included a trained nurse available for trips to and from homes and hospitals. The trained nurse was his wife Edna, who helped pioneer the business with him.

The Martin Funeral Home played an important part during the military disasters that occurred in San Joaquin

County during the 1940s. The first of these tragedies, during World War II, happened when an ammunition dump at Stockton Field's Army Air Corps Base exploded, killing 12 military personnel. The Air Corps had taken over the city's municipal airport as an advanced training base shortly before the United States entered the war. The Martin Funeral Home's involvement was a consequence of its contract with the government to direct funeral and burial arrangements for any military personnel deaths in San Joaquin County.

There was an even more devastating tragedy the night of November 16, 1949, when two B-29 bombers from an Air Force installation at Seattle—participating in a simulated air raid on Stockton— collided and crashed on McDonald Tract, a San Joaquin Delta area just west of Stockton. Nineteen crew members plunged to their deaths in the ill-fated planes and seven crew members parachuted to safety. As the functioning county coroner at the time (in those days the coroner's duties were rotated among the funeral homes of San Joaquin County) Martin Funeral Home took charge of the

bodies, assisted Air Force officers in identification, and arranged for shipment of the victims' bodies to their respective homes. This was the largest disaster occurring in San Joaquin County.

Martin Funeral Home has been extensively remodeled over the ensuing years; however, the small and intimate feeling remains intact. Its staff has quadrupled to 12 employees from the original operation. Upon Martin's death in 1978, the organization became Stockton's first all-female-owned mortuary: Daughter Jeanie Martin, a licensed funeral director, is president and manager; Edna Martin and another daughter, JoAnn Martin Thompson, serve as directors.

In reference to all-female mortuaries, Jeanie Martin stated in a recent newspaper interview, "I feel we are more sympathetic and less competitive, more caring and concerned with service."

KJOY-KJAX

If you ask Ort Lofthus what has kept his broadcast properties in a leadership role in Stockton for almost 30 years, he will undoubtedly give you a brief, concise answer: "Community involvement, consistency, and a competent, top-flight staff." Lofthus has been the head of KJOY-AM since 1953 and KJAX-FM since its inception in 1968. Both stations have maintained their own separate, consistent image under his guidance: KJOY with a contemporary sound, KJAX with an easy-listening music format.

"We fine-tune the programming now and then, but absolute consistency is a must for both stations," states Lofthus. Another ingredient for the broadcast properties' success has been extensive involvement with the community. The stations have taken up many important civic causes over the years,

among them the redevelopment of downtown Stockton, a mayoralty recall, and completion of "gaps" in the I-5 and Crosstown freeways.

Lofthus personally headed both of the freeway battles to their successful conclusion. He has devoted much of his time to schools and education,

local government, business groups, and organizations concerned with youth, women, and minorities. Often recognized for his leadership roles, he was named Young Man of the Year in 1959, and Mr. Stockton in 1969, and was paid special recognition by the state legislature in 1969 and by the San Joaquin Board of Supervisors in 1983.

"Of course, our leadership would never have happened without a staff of dedicated professionals," says Lofthus, pointing out that the employee tenure at his stations is the envy of the industry.

KJOY began operations as KXOB, from a Pacific Avenue location in 1947. It underwent several ownership changes until 1953, when Lofthus came to Stockton to head up its operation under the corporate name of Joseph Gamble Stations, Inc. The call letter change from KXOB to KJOY soon followed, along with a new programming format of contemporary music, news, and

sports, an identity retained today.

Its location had been changed to downtown Stockton in 1950 in the landmark Hotel Stockton. KJOY still broadcasts from its "window studios" at the corner of Weber and El Dorado. Lofthus became an owner and the corporation's president in

KJOY's attractive window studios have been a landmark in Stockton for more than 25 years. Over 40,000 automobiles pass by the facility daily.

1963 and put KJAX on the air in 1968, and in 1970 won a two-and-one-half-year battle for the city's cable television franchise (Big Valley Cablevision). KJAX is known as "Cloud 99" by many, because it began its operations featuring "heavenly music from atop the Medico-Dental Building."

Lofthus is the vice-president of the California Broadcasters' Association (the statewide radio, TV, and networks association). In his spare time he pilots a sailplane and prizes an international certificate for soaring to 25,000 feet. But his greatest satisfaction is his family. Lofthus' wife Sylvia is a registered nurse in administration at St. Joseph's Hospital. All four of their children and families reside in the Stockton area.

Ort Lofthus, civic-minded president and general manager of KJOY and KJAX.

BORELLI JEWELERS

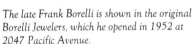

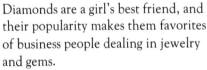

The late Frank Borelli is shown in the original Borelli Jewelers, which he opened in 1952 at 2047 Pacific Avenue.

Michael Borelli, a gemologist and son of the founder, is shown here with his wife Meg and their children, Dominic and Brenna.

Diamonds are a girl's best friend, and their popularity makes them favorites of business people dealing in jewelry and gems.

So avers Irene S. Borelli, operator of Borelli Jewelers, 2051 Pacific Avenue, one of Stockton's largest and finest retail jewelry stores. Irene is the widow of Frank M. Borelli, who founded the business in 1952 and continually operated the store until his death in 1976.

Born on a farm east of Stockton, Frank Borelli attended local schools, served in World War II, and received his degree in watchmaking from San Jose State University after the war. He was employed by a jewelry firm in Los Baños, California, from 1945 to 1947, subsequently purchasing the business which he operated until 1949. In 1952, after working for jewelry firms in San Jose and San Francisco, Borelli launched his own enterprise. He purchased Beers Jewelers, a small shop two doors south of the present location, and Borelli Jewelers came

into existence.

Initially the business was staffed by Frank Borelli and two salespersons. Patrons were offered costume jewelry and flatware as well as the fine jewelry and good service customers have come to identify with Borelli Jewelers.

The store was moved in 1965 to its present larger location at Pacific Avenue and Doris Place, where services and the selection of fine jewelry and precious gems were expanded.

Irene Borelli was born in Manchuria, where her father was engaged in the wholesale fur and jewelry business. The family immigrated to the United States when Irene was seven and established a wholesale pearl business, which continues today. Mrs. Borelli attended San Francisco schools, the University of California, and San Jose State University, receiving her degree in 1962. She maintained an active involvement in her family's business until her husband's death in 1976, when she assumed management of the store. Under Mrs. Borelli's direction, sales and services have continued to expand in the 3,000-square-foot store.

The organization now has a staff of 11, and provides numerous services including watch and jewelry repair, custom jewelry design and manufacture, appraisal and related gemological functions, as well as selling a wide variety of fine gems, jewelry, and watches.

Michael Borelli, son of the firm's founder, is Borelli's staff gemologist and assists in the store's management. Michael graduated from the University of San Francisco and served as a lieutenant in the United States Army for two years. He initially joined Borelli's in 1969, remained for three years, spent five years as a deputy probation officer, and returned to the family business permanently in 1978. Michael is a Registered Jeweler and Certified Gemologist, a member of the American Gem Society, and a graduate in residence of the internationally renowned Gemological Institute of America.

A. TEICHERT & SON, INC.

From cellar floors to superhighways, A. Teichert & Son, Inc., has provided a rock foundation for the growth of Central California.

The company has three major divisions. The Construction Division builds roads, freeways, underground utilities, canals, bridges, dams, parking lots, and playgrounds. The Aggregates Division produces gravel, sand, asphaltic and ready-mix concrete, and precast items. The Land Company develops building sites and leases land and buildings.

The venture started as a small family business in 1887. Adolph Teichert, a German immigrant, was foreman for the California Artificial Stone Paving Company. In his first advertisement he called himself "a manufacturer of artificial stone for sidewalks, garden walks, carriage drives, stable and cellar floors, fencing, coping, etc." Cement for this work came by ship in barrels from Belgium.

The founder's son, Adolph Jr., graduated with a degree in engineering from the University of California. He became a partner in 1912. Through his influence, the company took on larger, more complex jobs. Father and son worked together for the next 30 years. Together they helped organize the Northern California Chapter of the Associated General Contractors in 1915, and both participated in many civic and charitable activities.

To counter the effects of the Depression, the firm set up a gravel plant at Sacramento and introduced the use of ready-mix trucks. During the 1940s Teichert paved airfields and built revetments at Mather, McClellan, and Stockton Army Air Corps bases. It built dams in California, Oregon, and Nebraska,

Adolph Teichert, Sr., founder of A. Teichert & Son, Inc.

Adolph Teichert, Jr., joined his father's firm in 1912. Photo by Paul Kent.

worked on the Central Valley Water Project, and, locally, did construction for Rough and Ready Island, Pacific Avenue, Charter Way, University of the Pacific, and many residential and commercial projects, as well as major portions of I-5 and Highway 99 through the Stockton area.

The firm's Stockton office was opened in 1941 and currently employs 30 full-time people and 100 to 200 seasonal workers. A. Teichert & Son, Inc., maintains the oldest active contractor's license in the state of California, license number 8.

Adolph Teichert, Jr., had three sons, all connected with the business—Adolph III, Frederick, and Henry. Henry is now chairman of the board and Louis Riggs, a son-in-law, is president. Fred Teichert and Jud Riggs, great-grandsons of the company's founder, are also active in A. Teichert & Son, Inc. Many workers have given 20, 30, or

40 years of service and several are second-generation employees.

The company has changed over the years to keep pace with technological advances and complexities. It has developed imaginative ways to preserve resources, control air and noise pollution, and to be a good neighbor.

Today A. Teichert & Son, Inc., employs about 200 full-time people and 800 seasonal workers. It provides construction work and aggregates products to Northern and Central California. With headquarters in Sacramento in the beautifully land-scaped site of a reclaimed gravel plant, it also has district offices in Sacramento, Stockton, and Woodland, plus a sub-area office at Lake Tahoe. Teichert materials and labor have been responsible for a good share of the building of Central California.

HERMAN & HELEN'S MARINA

A 1983 rebuilding program provided Herman and Helen's Marina with 125 rental slips, a cafe, a store in a fiberglass barge, and allowed the doubling of the rental fleet.

Record-breaking rainfall in the winter of 1982-1983 caused a break in the Venice Island levee, flooding 3,000 acres of rich farmland and creating torrential river currents that swept away most of Herman and Helen's Marina on Little Connection Slough, 18 miles from Stockton by land and 16 miles by water.

Rushing through the break in November 1982, the current destroyed 155 slips, a cafe and store built on a concrete barge, and many boats, leaving intact only a shop and rental office. The strangest casualty was the barge-based cafe, which the current carried onto flooded Venice Island. Recovered and towed to a Stockton shipyard for repairs, the barge cafe broke up as it was being pulled from Stockton Channel into the shipyard.

In the center of the San Joaquin Delta's fishing, boating, and water skiing paradise, the marina started out in 1935 as a fishing resort operated by a "Shorty" Davis. Acquired by Herman and Helen Rauch in 1943, the resort was christened Herman and Helen's Marina, a name never changed despite several different ownerships.

The Rauches developed berthing and boating facilities and opened a cafe, for which Helen baked pies and made her special brand of chili. The husband-and-wife team retired in 1957, to be followed by a series of owners.

In 1973 Dave Smith, an avid boater and water skier and frequent Delta visitor, gave up his law practice in Sherman Oaks to join Jerry Matthews, an employee of the former owners, in a corporate venture to operate the 125-slip marina with Smith as president and manager and Matthews as secretary/treasurer.

Here's a year-by-year report on that operation:

1974—54 covered berths were acquired from the City of Stockton when a portion of McLeod's Lake was filled in for a Center Street crossing.

1975—The marina operators purchased the remainder of the fleet of houseboats started by George Ladd, who developed the conception of houseboats on the delta.

1975—The rental of ski boats was started.

1976—The gas dock was enlarged from 180 to 260 feet.

1977—The cafe was doubled and a store for groceries and marine supplies was added, a 900-square-foot shop was constructed, 16 open slips were built, but 20 covered berths were lost when the shed sank.

1978—The marina began providing camp-a-float services, allowing vacationers to drive their recreational vehicles onto motorized flatboats and cruise the delta with all the comforts of home.

1979—Nine open slips were added.

These expansions added up to a facility count of 24 houseboats, 12 ski boats, 12 camp-a-floats, 9 fishing boats, and 155 rental slips when disaster struck in 1982.

The 1983 rebuilding program provided 125 rental slips, a cafe built on a single urethane foam block, a store in a fiberglass barge, and allowed the doubling of the rental fleet. Herman & Helen's Marina also maintains a boat motor repair service and sells both new and used boats.

This 1981 aerial view shows Herman and Helen's Marina before it was damaged by strong river currents and high water the following year.

JOSEPH'S, INC., FURNITURE AND INTERIORS

Joseph's, Inc., Furniture and Interiors, provides design services as well as complete furnishings for home and office to its customers. Owner Joseph C. Jacobs believes his store, located at 2540 Pacific Avenue, offers "possibly the most elegant assembly of fine furniture anywhere."

The designer-businessman's early goals (at the prodding of his father) were to play football for the University of Santa Clara—and defeat arch-rival St. Mary's College—and later become a civil engineer. A star 146-pound halfback for St. Mary's High School, the Stockton native received a tentative football scholarship from University of the Pacific: It was contingent on his attending San Joaquin Delta College for one year, and putting on some 20 or 30 pounds.

However, a propensity and talent for interior design motivated the young man to enroll at Oakland's California College of Arts and Crafts, much to the chagrin of his father, following graduation from high school. Although they hardly spoke to each other for two years, the older man eventually became reconciled to his son's choice of career.

Graduating from the arts and crafts college in 1963, Jacobs worked for two years as an interior designer for Jackson's of Oakland. In 1965 he returned to Stockton and worked for

Owner Joseph C. Jacobs, who with three other designers creates personalized interior designs for both home and office.

Because of the elegance of Joseph's displays, they are often photographed by furniture manufacturers for use in their catalogs.

four months for a local furniture store, then opened Joseph's of Stockton—with a lone employee.

While Joseph's was a quality furniture store, the founder says, "I never made a cent." Therefore, he closed down in 1969 and, taking his inventory with him, became a designer for Jordan & Bowman. In 1973 the store changed to less design-oriented furniture in order to gain a larger-volume trade; at the same time the three partners of Jordan & Bowman opened an interior design studio at 944 West Robinhood, with Jacobs in charge.

After a year Jacobs purchased the operation, again hiring a lone employee, Kathleen Marshall, and in 1976 moved to St. Mark's Plaza—

renaming his company Joseph's, Inc., Furniture and Interiors. In December 1982 he joined with a building contractor for the construction of Avenue Galleria, a two-story, L-shaped business complex on Pacific Avenue. The store occupies two-thirds of the 9,000-square-foot complex, while other tenants are a ceramics-tile shop, an architectural firm, a women's fashion shop, and a hair stylist.

Today Joseph's handles all styles of furniture, conservative as well as elegant, and selects, designs, displays, and sells items suited to the nature and scheme of the office or home. The firm's four designers, including Jacobs, not only study building plans to ensure the furniture's compatibility, but often assist in designing the structures. They also sketch furnishings, to meet the customers' desires and needs, for furniture manufacturers.

Joseph's deals with some 700 furniture manufacturers, many of whom photograph the store's displays for use in their catalogs.

Joseph's, Inc., is located in the elegant Avenue Galleria on Pacific Avenue.

HOGAN MFG., INC.

In 1962 Walt Hogan, now chief executive officer, posed with his father Walter Sr., who founded Hogan Mfg., Inc.

Operating in the small town of Escalon does not deter the people of Hogan Mfg., Inc.—known in the trade as HMI—from thinking on a large scale basis.

A partial list of products the medium-size plant and structural-steel fabricating facilities build includes structural frames for industrial and commercial buildings; structural-steel tanks and bins; conveyors; stacks; ducts for power and fume control; stainless-steel plate work to specification, as well as cylindrical, panel, and general plate work; fan housings; scrubbers; and many types of mechanical equipment. The company's boundaries are not limited to manufacturing, however—it also provides field erecting crews to construct conveyors, modules, cast-in-place pipe machines, and giant cranes.

Outstanding among the buildings fabricated and erected by HMI are the imposing Gateway office complex in San Francisco, and the equally prominent RBJ Building at 15th and K streets in Sacramento. Another

endeavor HMI officials emphasize is the supersize cast-in-place concrete pipe machinery it constructed for the U.S. Air Force, which was used in the controversial MX missile tests.

The Escalon plant (located at 1704 First Street) averages around 300 employees, and has 220,000 square feet of shop space on 33 acres; a second plant in Phoenix, Arizona, has 150,000 square feet of operating space on 10 acres. The corporation's products—such as buildings, kilns, and bins—are erected on site.

Products manufactured in the Escalon and Phoenix operations are shipped nationally by truck and rail, as well as internationally out of the inland Port of Stockton (only 22 miles from Escalon). In total, the two factories manufacture some 5,000 tons of plate and structural steel monthly, with more than $40 million in sales realized annually in 1981 and 1982.

These huge figures began with $150,000 in sales and a staff of five—all part-owners—in 1944 when

Walter Hogan, Sr., and four comrade sheet-metal workers entered a partnership to operate the California Blowpipe and Steel Company.

Prior to the death of Walter Hogan, Sr., in 1967, his son Walt had acquired 90 percent of the company's stock and had become chief executive officer. During this period the name was changed to Hogan Mfg., Inc. HMI is now a third-generation operation; the successor's sons, Dale, Jeff, and Mark, are active in the concern.

Reminiscing back to the five founders of the original enterprise, Walt Hogan reminds that "all five had shop experience and no business experience, but were determined to fulfill their dreams of being in business for themselves and—well, make a profit—and grow with the times."

That same determination is apparent in the aspirations of today's Hogan Mfg., Inc.

This fabricated-steel, cast-in-place, concrete pipe machine was created by Hogan Mfg., Inc., for the U.S. Air Force for use in MX missile tests.

FREY DISTRIBUTING COMPANY

A German immigrant and one-time member of the German Junior Davis Cup tennis team, Hans Frey, was responsible in 1974 for saving the Anheuser-Busch (brewer of Budweiser and other beers in St. Louis since 1876) wholesalership for Stockton.

The city's distributorship had been operating at a loss for some time, and that year Anheuser-Busch was on the verge of discontinuing the operation.

The astute Frey, coordinator for the company's 11 nationwide wholesalerships, saw a potential in the area and decided to purchase the losing operation. At the time he took over what is now Frey Distributing Company, the Stockton-based wholesalership operated out of a small warehouse on Grimes Road with three trucks and a panel van. Annual sales were down to 150,000 cases, with a dollar value of about $600,000.

Zealously effecting many innovations, Frey brought the business back into the black in a few months; today the firm operates out of a distribution center with office space and a large refrigerated-storage area at 3932 Budweiser Court, Highway 99 and Waterloo Road. A staff of 50 is responsible for the sale and distribution of two million cases of "Bud" a year, with an annual dollar value of approximately $20 million.

The company's owner attributes his success to three factors: his wife Charlene, vice-president of finance and administration, who grew up with the company and at age 22 became California's first beer saleswoman; the "Big P" in business—better product, better people, and better pay; and Stockton—for its diversity in people, recreation, and progressive activity.

Appreciative that his adopted home has been good to him and his organization, Frey in turn is very community-minded. Frey Distributing Company is involved in the Bacon Bash, the annual benefit football game between the police and sheriff departments; the Stockton Children's Home benefit golf tournament; the Muscular Dystrophy Drive; the Mexican Cinco de Mayo Festival; and many other benefits and drives. Speaking frankly, he comments, "Such participation is not totally

unselfish—being a good corporate citizen is good for business."

The sports-minded former German Junior Davis Cup team member sponsors many amateur teams—and a few years ago saved the city's 30-year-old Captain Weber Days Regatta from extinction, after a local organization ceased sponsorship, by perpetuating the large boat-racing event as the Budweiser Western States Championship. Frey also assumed full sponsorship for Stockton's aspiring 1984 Olympic Games judoist, Tommy Martin, for which he was presented a plaque.

In 1983, after 103 years of brewing beer exclusively (and eight years of research), Anheuser-Busch began producing Master Cellars wine—Chablis, rosé, and Burgundy—in a Bakersfield winery.

Perhaps due to its successful Stockton operation, Frey Distributing Company in May 1983 was selected by Anheuser-Busch, Inc., to initiate commercial deliveries of the new wine, packaged in kegs, to cocktail lounges, restaurants, and similar establishments.

The San Joaquin County Board of Supervisors presented Hans Frey a plaque for his sponsorship of Tommy Martin (third from left), an Olympic judo aspirant. On Frey's right is Jose Alva, board chairman.

Hans Frey, president of Frey Distributing Company, and his wife and vice-president Charlene, who has the distinction of being California's first beer saleswoman.

DELTA OFFICE SYSTEMS AND FURNISHINGS, INC.

In addition to planning and designing office systems, Delta Office Systems and Furnishings, Inc., on St. Mark's Plaza, coordinates the decor and high-quality furnishings to tastefully enhance its clients' total office environment.

Founder William N. Highfill was almost constantly on the move before locating in Stockton. His corporate-executive father's every promotion dictated a family move: Tulsa, New York, St. Louis, then Houston. His nomadic life continued after graduation from Oklahoma State University in 1960 when, with a degree in marketing, the young man started as a sales trainee for Remington-Rand (manufacturer of business systems). Managerial positions led him to Chicago, Baltimore, Jacksonville, and finally San Francisco.

Therefore, Highfill was extremely interested when an opportunity arose in 1972 to go into business for himself in Stockton, where he could "keep my roots planted for the first time." Other selling points were that he liked Stockton because it was similar in size and environment to his hometown, and the business prospects were good. So Highfill purchased the operation of Edward Hunt, who in 1965 converted a Remington-Rand sales and service office (established in 1930, and for which Hunt had been district manager) into a franchise dealership for sales and service of filing systems, equipment, and microfilm systems known as Delta Office Systems and Machines.

Highfill made a slight but significant name change to Delta Office Systems and Furnishings, Inc.—stressing an office design and planning service, as well as sales of office furniture and fixtures. His

The furnishings and decor of Delta Office Systems and Furnishings, Inc., are good examples of open planning of office systems, a service provided by the company.

Tired of constantly being on the move as a sales manager, William N. Highfill settled in Stockton in 1972 and started his own business—Delta Office Systems and Furnishings, Inc.

business acumen is dedicated to "recommending the right product for the right job for the right interior at the right price." For example, Delta's design team first plans the business or commercial interior, fashioning the decor only after determining the type of business and the customer's particular needs and tastes.

Encompassing floor covering to ceiling, wall to wall, Delta office designs offer coordination of colors; different types of woodwork; plus recommendations for the most functional, practical, and convenient furniture and fixtures for each segment, or room, of the business. Highfill says the future of office systems lies in open planning, with free-standing partitions and modular work units—such as Delta's designer corner, in which open planning enables a 96-square-foot area to contain 42 feet of shelves, a rolltop desk, a lateral file cabinet, and a drafting table attached to a movable partition. The same in conventional furniture would require 250 square feet.

Delta collaborates with some 300 furniture manufacturers—and each year from 1977 to 1984 has won the Dealer Performance Award from Herman Miller, a leading manufacturer of open planning systems.

Highfill has participated in civic activities as a member of the executive committee and board of directors of The Greater Stockton Chamber of Commerce, president of the Administrative Management Society, and a member of the Yosemite Club and the Commercial Exchange Club.

CAMPBELL'S IN THE VILLAGE

Harry and Katie Campbell, the husband-and-wife team that founded Campbell's in the Village 30 years ago.

Name brands and high-fashion clothing and accessories for men, women, and children highlight Campbell's in the Village, at 21,000 square feet the largest retail store in Lincoln Center.

The operation began 30 years ago as a small children's clothing shop run by the husband-and-wife team of Harry and Katie Campbell.

Harry Campbell proved himself a born salesman when, as a young man in Roseburg, Oregon, he sold cherries and grapes at the local railroad station. But he shifted to ice cream cones when his developing business acumen told him that passengers preferred that delicacy.

Harry Campbell graduated from the University of Oregon with a degree in business administration, and Katie graduated from Oregon State University with a degree in home economics—specializing in clothing and art—and later taught clothing and textiles in Medford, Oregon.

The two met during interviews in a Portland department store. They both were subsequently hired as assistant buyers—Harry at JCPenney and Katie at Lipman Wolf. They later married and became business partners.

Harry rose to the position of manager in the store, and in 1949 the couple moved to Stockton, where Harry became assistant manager of a JCPenney store. The Campbells lived for two-and-one-half years in Stockton, and after a stint in Richmond returned here to stay.

Encouraged by developer Leroy Sims, a neighbor in Lincoln Village, tired of repeated relocations, and desiring to conduct their own business, the Campbells in 1953 opened a small children's clothing shop in Lincoln Center.

Later they added men's and women's clothing to their inventory and moved to their present site. Offering fashionable apparel and old-fashioned customer service, the store emphasizes quality merchandise that meets the needs of its middle-income customers.

Today Campbell's occupies this 21,000-square-foot store – the largest facility in Lincoln Center.

Because of his considerable experience in management over the years, Harry Campbell concentrates on the business operations of Campbell's in the Village, which bills itself as a specialty department store. Katie, with her expertise in clothing, textiles, and fabrics, serves as fashion advisor.

Stressing the store's personal touch, Katie Campbell says, "We treat our customers as though they were guests in our homes." The friendliness of the staff also is emphasized by Harry Campbell, who states, "We try to think of our group as one large family doing the best job we can."

Today Campbell's in the Village is incorporated, with operations directed by Harry Campbell, chairman of the board; Terry Cossette, president and merchandise manager of the women's department; and Carroll Caminata, store manager and merchandise manager of the men's and children's departments.

Although the Campbells are now semiretired, Harry Campbell drops in the store almost daily "just to keep in touch."

STOCKTON PATRONS

The following individuals, companies, and organizations have made a valuable commitment to the quality of this publication. Windsor Publications and the Greater Stockton Chamber of Commerce gratefully acknowledge their participation in *Stockton: Sunrise Port on the San Joaquin.*

Acme Truck Parts and Equipment, Inc.*
  Acme Truck Lifts, Inc.
Dr. Ron and Cynthia Allison
Alpine Packing Company*
American Honda Motor Co., Inc.
Babka Beer Company*
Bank of America, Stockton Offices
Don Blair Lumber Co.*
Borelli Jewelers*
The Builders' Exchange of Stockton, Inc.
California Cedar Products Company*
Campbell's in the Village*
Computerland of Stockton
Connell Motor Truck Company*
Corn Products*
County Wide Yellow Pages
Edmund S. "Ed" Coy
Day and Night Locks and Security
  Systems*
Delicato Vineyards
Delta Office Systems and Furnishings, Inc.*

Diehl, Steinheimer, Riggio, Haydel and
  Mordaunt
FranRica Manufacturing, Inc.*
Frantz Filter Company*
  Lois Yee Cosmetics, Inc.
Freeman, Rishwain & Hall*
Frey Distributing Company*
Froeliger Machine Tool Company*
Geiger Manufacturing Company*
The Grupe Companies
Herman and Helen's Marina*
Hickinbotham Bros. Ltd.*
Hogan Mfg., Inc.*
Holt Bros.*
Home Environment Care
Loyal and Jean Hutchison
Joseph's Inc., Furniture and Interiors*
Michel G. Khoury M.D., Inc.
KJOY-KJAX*
Oscar Budd Kleinfeld and Co.
Martin Funeral Home*
Robert J. Meath-Franklin Life Insurance
  Co.
Moorman Mfg. Co. of California, Inc.
Dr. James Morrissey
Moss, Craig and Wiggins Commercial Real
  Estate, Inc.
Nuemiller and Beardslee*
On Lock Sam's*

Pollardville*
Quinn's Books
Dr. and Mrs. Joseph A. Redding
H.H. Robertson Company
T.A. Ross - Collections
St. Joseph's Hospital*
San Joaquin County Museum Docent
  Council
San Joaquin Lumber Company
SDI Community Developers*
Shepherd and Green*
Dr. and Mrs. William E. Shinn
Stockton Inn*
Stockton Orthopedic Medical Group, Inc.
Sumiden Wire Products Corporation
A. Teichert and Son, Inc.*
Termite Control Company, Inc.
University of the Pacific, Office of
  Development
Valimet, Inc.*
Valley Electric Company*
Mary Wilkinson, M.D.
Henry Wolters and Son

*Partners in Progress of *Stockton: Sunrise Port on the San Joaquin.* The histories of these companies and organizations appear in Chapter 8, beginning on page 117.

SELECTED BIBLIOGRAPHY

Allen, Glen, and Young, Chas. H. *Architecture.* Stockton, Ca.: Monograph, 1929.

Bailey, Edgar H. *"Geology of Northern California."* San Francisco: Bulletin 190, U.S. Geological Survey (1966), California Div. of Mines.

Bancroft, Hubert Howe. *California Pioneer Register.* Baltimore: Regional Publishing, 1964.

Barrett, S.A., and Gifford, E.W. *Miwok Natural Culture.* Yosemite National Park, Ca.: Yosemite Natural History Association, 1959.

Bennyhoff, James Allen. *Ethnogeography of the Plains Miwok.* Davis, Ca.: University of California at Davis, 1977.

Bryant, Edwin. *What I Saw In California.* Santa Ana, Ca.: The Fine Arts Press, 1936.

Cook, Sherburne F. *"The Aboriginal Population of the San Joaquin Valley California,"* Berkeley and Los Angeles, Ca.: Anthropological Records, Vol. 16 (No. 2), University of California Press, Berkeley, 1955.

———. *"Expeditions to the Interior of California's Central Valley from 1820-1840."* Berkeley and Los Angeles, Ca.: Vol. 20 (No. 5), Anthropological Records. University of California Press, 1962.

Derbec, Erienne. *A French Journalist in California.* Georgetown, Ca.: Edited by A.P. Nasatire. Talisman Press, 1964.

Dillion, Richard. *Fool's Gold: Captain John Sutter.* Santa Cruz, CA.: Western Tanager, 1967.

Duran, Narcisco. *Diary of Fray Narcisco Duran: Expedition on the Sacramento and San Joaquin Rivers in 1817.* Berkeley, Ca.: University of California, 1911.

Gilbert, F.T. *History of San Joaquin County.* Oakland, Ca.: Thompson & West, 1879.

Grunsky, Carl Ewald. *Stockton Boyhood.* Berkeley, Ca.: Friends of the Bancroft Library, 1959.

Gunter, Elder. *The City of Stockton: Past, Present & Future.* Stockton, Ca.: Private Printing, 1977.

Hammond, George, and Morgan, Dale.

Captain Charles M. Weber. Berkeley, Ca.: The Friends of the Bancroft Library, 1966.

Hartmann, Ilka. *The Youth Charles M. Weber, Founder of Stockton.* Stockton, Ca.: University of the Pacific, 1979.

Hollembeak, J.R. *A History of the Public Schools of Stockton California.* Stockton, Ca.: Private Printing, 1909.

Hutchinson, W.H. *California, The Golden Shore by the Sundown Sea.* Palo Alto, Ca. Star Publishing, 1980.

Johnson, Herbert B. *Discrimination Against the Japanese in California.* Berkeley, Ca.: R&E Research Association, 1971.

Kennedy, Glen. *It Happened in Stockton.* Stockton, Ca.: Private Printing, 1967.

Kroeber, A.L. *Handbook of the Indians of California.* Berkeley, Ca.: California Book Company, 1952.

———. *"Yokuts Dialect Survey."* Berkeley, Ca.: Anthropological Records, Vol. 11 (No. 3), University of California Press, 1961.

Latta, F.F. *Handbook of Yokuts Indians.* Bakersfield, Ca.: Kern County Museum, 1949.

Lyman, George D. *John Marsh, Pioneer.* New York: Charles Scribners Sons, 1930.

Maloney, Alice Bay. *Fur Brigade to the Bonaventura: John Works California Expedition 1832-1833.* San Francisco, Ca.: California Historical Society, 1945.

Margolin, Malcolm. *The Ohlone Way.* Berkeley, Ca.: Heyday Books, 1978.

———. *The Way We Lived.* Berkeley, Ca.: Heyday Books, 1981.

McAfee, Ward. *California Railroad Era, 1850-1911.* San Marino, Ca.: Golden West Books, 1973.

McComb, Delmar M., Jr. *The City of Great Peace.* Stockton, Ca.: Private Printing, 1961.

———. *Beat! Beat! Drums!, A History of Stockton During the Civil War.* Stockton, Ca.: Private Printing, 1965.

Miller, William J. *California Through the Ages.* Los Angeles, Ca.: Westernlore Press, 1957.

Minnick, Sylvia Sun. *Chinese in San Joaquin County.* Sacramento, Ca.: Thesis, Sacramento State University, 1983.

Norris, Robert Matheson, and Webb, Robert W. *Geology of California.* New York: Wiley, 1976.

Oakeshott, Gordon B. *California's Changing Landscape.* New York: McGraw Hill, 1978.

Pellegrini, Albert. *Stockton's Reaction to Europe and Mexican Involvement 1914-1918.* Stockton, Ca.: Thesis, San Joaquin Delta College History 10, 1973.

Penrose, Eldon R. *California Nativism: Organized Opposition to Japanese, 1890-1913.* San Francisco: Reprint, R&E Research Association, 1973.

Ragir, Sonia. *The Early Horizon in Central California Prehistory.* Berkeley, Ca.: University of California, Department of Anthropology, 1972.

Roberts, James Arthur. *Stockton Manufacturing.* San Jose, Ca.: Smith & McKay Printing, 1978.

Taylor, Bayard. *Eldorado or Adventure in the Path of an Empire.* New York: G.P. Putnam, 1868.

Taylor, Clotilde Grunsky. *Dear Family.* Stockton, Ca.: Private Printing, 1929.

Tinkham, George H. *History of San Joaquin County, California.* Los Angeles: Historic Record Company, 1923.

Winther, Ocsar O. *Express and Stagecoach Days in California.* Palo Alto, Ca.: Stanford University Press, 1936.

———. Works Progress Administration of the City of Stockton. *History of San Joaquin County.* Stockton, Ca.: Private Printing, 1938.

INDEX